The Forest Deep

An Epic Business Fable

By
Gaylen K. Bunker

Printed in The United States of America

BusinessAllstars

Introduction

The ancient Phoenician we're some of the first traveling merchants who took their wares by ship throughout the Mediterranean. They encountered many countries and peoples that employed languages that were foreign to them, used pictographs, cuneiforms, and hieroglyphics in addition to roman numerals as their written communication methods. These all seemed cumbersome and not very easily understood. So they introduced a much simpler method: An alphabet of letters representing sounds that could be used in combination to make words and a Hindu/Arabic numbering system.

This technological advance was met by some with skepticism if not superstitious disdain. But eventually, people saw the wisdom of a more easily usable method that common traders could learn and would greatly facilitate commerce. As a result of many years of refinement western civilization arrived at what we now know as English. Codified by William Tyndale in his first published English Bible in 1537, many of the spellings have continued since that time.

Evidently, in Tyndale's time there was widespread use of the digraph "gh" embedded in words that represented a voiceless velar fricative or consonantal sound. In the intervening years this sound appears to have been lost, but we still have the residual "gh" spread throughout the language for no apparent reason. In an effort to streamline the language and make it more commercially usable the inhabitants of Forest Deep and surrounding areas have eliminated it and never use 'gh' together in a word.

All of the words where 'gh' would appear have a more phonetic spelling. They do use the rule that for a vowel to have a long sound, it must be followed immediately by an 'e'. Some examples of the changes are: high is hie; bright is briet; fight is fiet; light is liet; might is miet; night is niet; right is riet; sight is siet; tight is tiet; straight is straet; and weight is waet. In the case of 'ough,' the new spelling is either 'aw', 'oe', 'ue', or 'uff' and thought is thawt; though is thoe; through is thrue; enough is enuf; and so forth.

It's just more natural.

The reader is asked not only to read about efficiency and growth as applied to valuation, but to experience it first hand in this change in the language. The book also asks the reader to accept new dimensions and ideas through the metaphor of a fable. Change is never easy, but I can assure you, it is worth it. From this point forward no "gh" will appear.

Gaylen K. Bunker

Acknowledgements

I want to express appreciation for the generous contributions made by my wife, Diane, who has read and reread the manuscript many times and given extremely valuable input. I would also like to thank the many students through the years that have offered suggestions and encouragement.

Gaylen K. Bunker

Table of Contents

The Wizard of g

(An Epic Business Fable)

Monday – June 1

Once upon a time, in a world of abstraction and metaphor, a Rabbit with unusually large ears lived in a tree-hollow cottage nestled in Forest Deep. The Deep was a vast expanse of lush timber and vegetation in a broad valley between Rocky Ridge and the Great Sand Bar. Meandering thrue the trees along the valley floor was Mill Stream, a crystal clear fountain of water.

The most notable feature of Forest Deep was a clearing where Mill Stream dumped into Beggar's Pond, the collection point that provided the stored energy to turn a large wooden wheel. The rhythm of the wheel rumbled thrue a massive clapboard structure with an imposing sign that read: Red Maple Mill. Not far from the mill was Gnarly Oak, whose limbs reached majestically outward, filling the rest of the clearing. The tree served as a central gathering place for all important events in Forest Deep.

Red Maple Mill had been constructed long years ago to utilize the power from Mill Stream. It was not only the main source of occupation for all the inhabitants of Forest Deep, but the community social center.

Rabbit was up early because today there was to be a very important meeting of the directors of Red

Maple Mill. Each of the directors also served as officers in the enterprise and met periodically to decide major issues concerning operations of Red Maple Mill. They were all to be assembled around Gnarly Oak when the rays from the early morning sun first fell on the leaves that projected from the uppermost branches of the surrounding trees. As usual, today they were to receive instructions from Owl, their wondrous leader. Rabbit was excited because it was always a special event to be with Owl and see how he managed the affairs of Red Maple Mill.

On his way to the meeting, Rabbit stopped to see if Skunk and Raccoon were ready. Skunk lived not far from Rabbit down a crooked lane at Hallow Haven Lodge, and Raccoon was just a little further in Brownwood Cottage. As soon as Skunk saw Rabbit coming, she casually called thrue her window, "I'm coming, I'm coming, don't get your ears in a twist!" This was typical of Skunk's attitude about everything. She seemed to be the most carefree member of the board.

"Let's go. I'm sure Raccoon will be waiting," Rabbit encouraged. He had intentionally come early to get Skunk moving, so they could hopefully be on time. When they got to Raccoon's cottage, he was anxiously pacing the porch.

"Let me take this opportunity to say how glad I am that you are both ready," Raccoon said sarcastically. The word 'opportunity' was most appropriate, for Raccoon liked to take advantage when ever possible.

As the three approached Gnarly Oak, they could see that most of the other members were already there. Gander was stretching his neck hie into the air and looking everywhere to see who was present. Porcupine was just outside the circle, keeping her usual solitary distance from everyone. Fox was meticulously checking off each member as they arrived, and Ferret was quietly perched on a log carefully watching the others. Gander turned his head from side to side to survey the situation and reported, "I think we're all here."

"That's riet. I count seven of us," noted Fox.

As Rabbit, Skunk, and Raccoon were settling into place, Gander pointed into the sky and announced: "Here he comes!" Everyone looked up to see a magnificent spread-winged bird soar hie above and gradually descend toward them. It was inspiring to see Owl in his commanding approach. He gracefully came to rest on his usual perch on one of the large lower limbs of the tree. Slowly Owl turned his head from side to side, surveying each of the board members carefully to see if everyone was in their place, and found that all were ready for the meeting. Then he began.

"Welcome to a most critical meeting of the board. The Mill has done fairly well these past few years under my leadership, but times are changing. I've decided to retire, which means I will not be able to continue as your chairman in the future."

All were shocked at this sudden turn of events, but dared not interrupt Owl as he continued his remarks: "Therefore, I will be coordinating the appointment of a successor to oversee operations. One of you will be the new leader. I've personally chosen each of you for your current positions and know of your strengths and weaknesses. I'm proud of you all and the diversity the board represents. The new leader will have to take on the responsibility of charting a new direction for Red Maple Mill."

"I've decided to make this a competition with the final decision based on which of you can correctly solve a riddle. I will return in one week's time and want an answer to the following question -- What is the value of Red Maple Mill? It's not just the answer that I'm looking for, but the methodology and philosophy you use to explain your answer. Are there any questions?"

The board members all sat in stunned silence. They had relied on Owl's leadership for a long time and the prospect of change seemed extremely unsettling. They each looked around at the others, trying to envision who miet be able to take his place. Who could assume the awesome responsibility as their new leader?

"What do you mean by the value of Red Maple Mill?" Rabbit reluctantly asked, hoping not to show his ignorance.

"That is part of the puzzle, to define value and tell what it is," was Owl's response.

The directors looked at each other curiously, wondering about the assignment. Then Owl added: "One of you will be transformed and thrue this process will become what I will refer to as the 'Wizard of g.' I've added the 'g' to this title for a very specific reason that will only become apparent at some later time. As you search, it will become obvious who in fact has the capability to coordinate the efforts to fiet the dragons this enterprise faces."

Dragons---the directors each tried to make sense of what was being said. What dragons?

"I'll be back in one week," Owl said. With that he spread his powerful wings, and with a sliet jump was airborne. He circled the group, looked at each one, then turned his head skyward, caut an updraft, and slowly ascended into the brilliant sky.

"I don't think I'm a wizard," whispered Skunk to Rabbit and Raccoon. "I don't know what it would feel like, but I don't think it feels the way I feel."

"Yea, I don't think you're a wizard either," added Raccoon.

"Well, do you think you are?" an incredulous Skunk shot back at Raccoon.

"Who knows? Maybe I am," Raccoon announced as he swirled his arms in the air as if to create magic out of the nothingness.

Then the two looked at Rabbit, who seemed to be deep in thawt. "What's wrong with you?" asked Skunk.

"I feel like a fool. I'm the only one who posed a question and I looked stupid. Everyone probably knows what value is, except me," Rabbit muttered.

"Why it's, it's---I don't know," Skunk stammered.

Raccoon, seizing the opportunity to show his superior grasp of the situation and feeling that he was stating the obvious said:

'***It's the price someone would pay to purchase the business***.'"

"Wow, you must be the wizard," uttered a stunned Skunk, looking at Raccoon.

"You mean someone wants to buy Red Maple Mill?" Rabbit asked.

"Why else would Owl want to know what it is worth?" Raccoon responded.

"Gee," said Skunk.

"But Owl didn't exactly say price, he said value," corrected Rabbit.

"Price---value, what's the difference? When it comes time to sell, they're the same thing," Raccoon responded.

"I'm not so sure of that. I've often acquired something that had great value to me for a price which was much lower. Then again I've paid much more for something that turned out to be worth much less. There is always the problem of anticipation versus realization."

“Do you remember the time I went to Bushy Meadow? I had to buy supplies for Red Maple Mill and Gopher accompanied me. My, he was a very talented negotiator. I remember how he assessed the situation, the seller, and the products. By the time he was thrue, we ended up paying way below what I thawt those supplies were worth. That incident told me there was a major difference between price and value,” said Rabbit.

“Yea, but those were supplies, a relatively benign commodity,” Raccoon continued. We are talking about a whole enterprise that is fairly complex. On the one hand we have the value of supplies and resources coming to Red Maple Mill, and on the other hand we have the value of the added labor and technology to convert them into finished products. There is a big difference between simple supplies and the enterprise we know as Red Maple Mill. The only way to really know the value of Red Maple Mill is to put it up for sale and see what a willing buyer would pay.”

Rabbit marveled at Raccoon’s grasp of the situation, but somehow he just couldn’t see Raccoon as having all the answers. Even thoe the company was much more complex than a group of supplies, it still seemed there was justifiable reason to assume there was a difference between price and value.

Suddenly, Skunk interrupted. “I wonder why Owl referred to the new leader as the Wizard of g? What is so special about g? If we are to figure out what the

value of the Company is, why not determine the Wizard of v?"

Rabbit was shocked. He had written off Skunk as a contender for the title because of her apparent carefree attitude. Even thoe Rabbit disagreed with Raccoon, he had a lot of respect for Raccoon's thinking, but this was a surprisingly astute question on Skunk's part. Maybe he had underestimated Skunk. "That's a great question. I also wonder what g represents," Rabbit responded.

That niet Rabbit made a list of all the board members and how he perceived them:

Skunk is easy-going, but deceptively deep.

Raccoon is an opportunist who takes advantage whenever possible.

Gander is always looking to see the big picture.

Fox is meticulous and analytical.

Ferret is creative and innovative.

Porcupines is defensive and ever on guard for potential risk.

Rabbit wondered--who am I? Thoe I'm not the youngest in actual age I'm probably the newest board member. I've only been at Red Maple Mill for a couple of years, having spent several years as an information officer at Prairie Gardens. With my ear to the ground, I listen and gather information that is often processed by others. Maybe it is time to collect

all the information available and then--then--process it myself.

Rabbit decided that starting the next morning he would visit each director in turn and determine who they thawt was the most logical candidate to be the Wizard of g. If he appeared to be no threat, then perhaps they would share some of their wisdom with him. Rabbit retired for the niet.

Tuesday – June 2

The next day Rabbit arrived at Gander's home about mid-morning. He didn't want to appear to be too anxious--that could send a bad signal. Gander was enjoying a morning swim in his own private pool. He seemed to be deep in thawt when Rabbit approached. "Am I interrupting you?" Rabbit called out from the bank.

"Not a bit. I've just been ruminating concerning what Owl said yesterday. It will be good to have someone to discuss things with." Gander swam over to the edge of the pool, slowly walked out, and fluffed a bit to shake off the water.

"I think that you are someone who sees the big picture. You have a wonderful point of view. Why do you think value is so important?" Rabbit asked.

"It seems to me that it has implications for everyone associated with Red Maple Mill," Gander answered.

Rabbit questioned: "What do you mean everyone?"

"By everyone, I mean those who provide resources, those who make products, and even those who purchase the products. I think everyone wants to be connected to something that is alive and doing well. Value has to reflect the health and prosperity of Red Maple Mill," Gander stated.

"It's interesting that you put it in terms of 'alive' and 'healthy.' The Company almost sounds more organic than financial," Rabbit mused out loud.

"From my point of view the single biggest issue in all of commerce is the relationship between benefits and costs. A business is much more than numbers on a report. We summarize revenues or benefits and do the same with expenses or costs. We subtract one from the other and the difference tells us if we are ahead of the game or behind it."

Gander continued: "In business you must manage the costs so that you can generate a product or service that is the best it can be, given those costs. You don't want to spend too little and have poor quality, or spend too much and be wasteful. A good manager will control costs appropriately."

"The real trick is the revenues," Gander said as he drew a triangle on the ground. "In a totally free market with lots of competition it is hard to price your product or service so that you can enjoy a sufficient markup over costs. The bottom of this triangle represents a free market where everyone competes aggressively. Margins are low and earnings are meager."

"The point on the triangle, opposite from the base where competition is fierce, represents a pure monopoly position. Here there are few competitors and you have the freedom to set prices. Most businesses strive to be in this position, but it is difficult."

"What do you mean?" Rabbit asked.

"You have to separate yourself from the crowd in some way so that customers are driven to your product at the exclusion of all others."

"How does that happen?" Rabbit queried.

"I can think of four ways for a company to put themselves in that kind of exclusive position. First is RESOURCES, where a company has superior financing, equipment, contractual arrangements, and workforce to all others. Second is RESEARCH, where a company has proprietary knowledge about the product, production, or the market that others don't have. The third would be REPUTATION, where the customers choose a company's products, above all others, because of loyalty to the brand as the result of past experience, familiarity, or status. Last is REGULATION, where customers have no alternative and are required to give their trade to a particular company. The more that a company can move toward an exclusive monopoly position, the more freedom they have to set prices and realize healthy profits. In most cases customers will pay for superior value," Gander summarized.

"Owl has often said that wealth is the baggage of valued service. That sounds very similar." Rabbit concluded.

Gander then related the following story:

The Orange Grove

Badger once owned an orange grove. He worked very hard to make it a first class operation and produced the very best oranges. As a result of his labors, his oranges were preferred to all others, they sold at premium prices, and the enterprise earnings were very strong. He worked for many years to build up an excellent operation.

As time went on, Badger grew tired and wanted to relax and enjoy his last few years in retirement. He decided to retain ownership of the grove and hire a manager to run things. He interviewed many candidates, but Weasel appeared energetic and briet, so he was hired.

As soon as Badger had moved away, Weasel began to change how the grove was operated. He felt there were too many expensive procedures that could be trimmed. Other 'efficiencies' were implemented, and before he knew it the first crop of oranges was ready for picking. However, the oranges were not of the same quality that had been produced previously, and Weasel was fearful that sales would be poor.

He learned from a competitor that oranges could be 'improved' by injecting them with water to make them heavier and dying the outside a beautiful, healthy, consistent orange color. The oranges appeared to be better than ever and a lot of people purchased them. Sales that first year were wonderful.

Badger was living some distance away and unaware of what was going on. Now, the interesting thing is the communication. Weasel sent a report to Badger that sales were terrific, earnings were up, and a nice check would be coming. Badger was very pleased.

The second year, after 'perfecting' the oranges as he had done before, sales were poor. No one returned to buy that year. But Weasel was very clever. He enjoyed the reward of operating the grove and wanted to stay as long as he could, so he decided that since Badger had no first-hand knowledge of what was happening, the easiest thing to do was to send a false report. Weasel thawt that Badger would never know.

Weasel reported that sales were even better than the previous year and earnings were up. He knew that Badger would expect a healthy portion of the earnings be sent to him, so he concocted a plan. He sent a letter to Badger telling him that since sales had increased so much, he would need to plow most of the earnings back into the operations for expansion to cover future demand.

Weasel had learned that records can indeed be manipulated to hide reality.

Badger reluctantly agreed and was deceived.

"I can't believe that anyoı Rabbit seemed amazed.

"It happens all the time," c("Most managers are not quite t do a little shuffling of the numb ruff years and make the earning rate, instead of vacillating up an

"Sounds like being loosey G numbers," responded Rabbit.

"It could even result in a wild those who rely on the numbers." and then chuckled at the reference

"You've had a lot of experienc you are on the board. So in your m value that Owl is looking for?" Ral

Rabbit's apparent lack of experi at ease and he felt comfortable disc challenge. "In my mind the whole tl to earnings: Is the bottom line legitiı manipulation, and will it continue in Value is a direct result of earnings cc strong sales, which are in turn a resul of the product."

"Is that it?" queried Rabbit.

"Almost. If the numbers are good, used as a basis for the calculation of va said.

"How do you know if the numbers a

"I have ten questions that I ask," res Gander.

1. Does "Net Income" translate into cash flow?
2. Is revenue growth fully explained?
3. Is there a lot of non-operating activity?
4. Are estimates and accruals reasonable?
5. Are the external auditors free to do their job?
6. Are financial ratios consistent over time?
7. Are "Internal Controls" a hie priority?
8. Is there any reason to doubt management?
9. Are "Related Party Transactions" fully disclosed?
10. Are receivables, inventory, and payables solid?

Gander did not want to disclose his entire ethod, so he left it there.

"Wow. I never realized it could be so omplicated. I was looking for something a little asier to understand," Rabbit puzzled.

"Well, aside from making sure the numbers are good, you need to try the product," replied Gander. "If Badger had been in a position to sample the end product he would have known instantly something was wrong. This gets back to one of the intangibles – try the product."

"That certainly sounds like an impressive theory, and I wouldn't be a bit surprised to see you selected as the Wizard of g," Rabbit confessed.

When Rabbit left Gander, he swung by Ferret's home to see if he was there. Ferret didn't want to talk riet then. He told Rabbit to come back the next day, sometime after breakfast. They agreed to meet then.

"I can't believe that anyone would do that." Rabbit seemed amazed.

"It happens all the time," conceded Gander. "Most managers are not quite that blatant, they just do a little shuffling of the numbers to smooth out the ruff years and make the earnings increase at a steady rate, instead of vacillating up and down."

"Sounds like being loosey Goosey with the numbers," responded Rabbit.

"It could even result in a wild Goose chase for those who rely on the numbers." They both paused and then chuckled at the references.

"You've had a lot of experience. I can see why you are on the board. So in your mind what is the value that Owl is looking for?" Rabbit asked.

Rabbit's apparent lack of experience put Gander at ease and he felt comfortable discussing the challenge. "In my mind the whole thing comes down to earnings: Is the bottom line legitimate, free from manipulation, and will it continue into the future? Value is a direct result of earnings coming from strong sales, which are in turn a result of the quality of the product."

"Is that it?" queried Rabbit.

"Almost. If the numbers are good, they can be used as a basis for the calculation of value," Gander said.

"How do you know if the numbers are good?"

"I have ten questions that I ask," responded Gander.

1. Does “Net Income” translate into cash flow?
2. Is revenue growth fully explained?
3. Is there a lot of non-operating activity?
4. Are estimates and accruals reasonable?
5. Are the external auditors free to do their job?
6. Are financial ratios consistent over time?
7. Are “Internal Controls” a hie priority?
8. Is there any reason to doubt management?
9. Are “Related Party Transactions” fully disclosed?
10. Are receivables, inventory, and payables solid?

Gander did not want to disclose his entire method, so he left it there.

“Wow. I never realized it could be so complicated. I was looking for something a little easier to understand,” Rabbit puzzled.

“Well, aside from making sure the numbers are good, you need to try the product,” replied Gander. “If Badger had been in a position to sample the end product he would have known instantly something was wrong. This gets back to one of the intangibles – try the product.”

“That certainly sounds like an impressive theory, and I wouldn’t be a bit surprised to see you selected as the Wizard of g,” Rabbit confessed.

When Rabbit left Gander, he swung by Ferret’s home to see if he was there. Ferret didn’t want to talk riet then. He told Rabbit to come back the next day, sometime after breakfast. They agreed to meet then.

That niet Rabbit tried to piece together all he had learned. The day before, Raccoon said that price was based on what someone would pay for Red Maple Mill, which was the same as its value. Rabbit had a sense that price and value were different and so could not buy into Raccoon's conclusion.

Then there was everything that Gander had said. Could it be that the financial reports from a lot of enterprises were inaccurate? It seemed that to Gander, value was the reliability of the reported earnings, and that was a direct result of the quality of the operations. Rabbit went to his cupboard and pulled out copies of the last several reports issued by Red Maple Mill to examine them more closely. They looked good to him. Then he thawt about the last thing Gander said -- 'Try the oranges.' The shingles that were produced at Red Maple Mill were excellent. Rabbit knew this from first-hand knowledge. Rabbit had spent a lot of time with Beaver, who was foreman of Red Maple Mill. He even shingled his own house. The numbers had to be good.

Wednesday – June 3

The next day, before Rabbit went to see Ferret he stopped by Red Maple Mill to visit with Beaver, the Chief Operating Officer. Perhaps he could learn more about value by seeing operations first hand.

As he walked into Red Maple Mill, Beaver and others were scurrying around. When Beaver saw

Rabbit, he motioned for another to take over directing operations and greeted Rabbit. "It's always good to see a member of the board. Is there anything I can do for you?"

"I'm trying to get a better understanding of things," Rabbit stated. "To be perfectly blunt, I'm trying to determine what the value of Red Maple Mill is. I have the greatest respect for your operational leadership and wondered what you think gives Red Maple Mill value."

"Is there someone interested in purchasing Red Maple Mill?" Beaver wanted to know.

"No, I don't think that is a consideration at this point. I think it is just an exercise to help focus the members of the board and get us thinking."

Beaver mused for a moment as he looked around and then said: "I've thawt about this a lot and I think value comes down to leadership and unlocking stakeholder potential." Beaver motioned for Rabbit to follow him as he started toward a small office in one corner of the mill.

Rabbit was quick to pick up on Beaver's lead and the two entered the small room. As they did Rabbit surveyed the efficient work area with an old wooden desk and two chairs. Beaver motioned for Rabbit to sit down as he moved to the other chair. "I think value is dependent on leadership and if you don't mind I'd like to tell you my theory of leadership," Beaver began.

"Please go ahead," Rabbit encouraged. "I'd love to hear it."

The fourth woodchuck

Beaver continued: "I saw that each of them had a flaw, but also realized that all of us have those same flaws at one time or another. We all can serve, listen, and deliberate depending on the situation. The question became: which woodchuck was least handicapped by their own flaw? Could the self-serving woodchuck serve the company's greater good? Could the know-it-all woodchuck listen to advice from others? Could the impulsive woodchuck be more rational and thawtful? As I was struggling with this dilemma a fourth woodchuck that I had never considered came to my attention. Her quiet steadiness had not seemed assertive enuf, but the more I thawt about her the better I felt. She exemplified unselfish service to the organization, she listened and learned from others, and she approached decisions with very controlled emotion. She also had great integrity."

"The only problem was: her management style was very different than mine. I'm generally hierarchical with clear lines of authority, while she is very open and inclusive. I ultimately promoted her to the second position and she worked out to be excellent."

"It is critical to have solid leadership at every level in the organization. I have worked many years to fill the ranks with competent and trusted employees. I'm not always successful, because just as soon as I find an excellent leader, they move on to greater opportunity. It is a little frustrating. Some leaders try to hold their best subordinates back, which I find to be counterproductive. I wish I could say we were as strong as I would hope."

"Are you saying we could do better?" Rabbit asked.

"Let me say we have come a long way and are on the road to progress. I'm very comfortable with all that we've done and proud of our accomplishments, but there is always room for more. I'd be short sieted if I didn't think we could continue to do better," Beaver said.

"I appreciate your honesty. You mention integrity in your list and I can see that you really mean it."

"I think it is the cornerstone of any business."

"I'm on my way to see another board member and I don't want to keep you from your work. May I come again and discuss this further?" Rabbit inquired.

"I always have time for anyone truly interested in Red Maple Mill. I'd be glad to see you again," Beaver ended.

Rabbit thawt about what Beaver had to say as he proceeded to Ferret's home. Finally, he arrived at his destination and greeted Ferret who was just returning to his home.

After a short greeting Rabbit began: "Ferret, I really respect you as a member of the board and the contribution you make."

Ferret seemed a little cautious. "I'm glad to hear you say that, because I'm not sure everyone agrees."

"It seems like you always have the most creative ideas even thoe you don't usually get the credit," Rabbit continued.

"I hope it is apparent that others are always trying to take credit for the ideas that I come up with."

"I think it is. It certainly is to me," Rabbit consoled. "Ever since Owl announced the competition, I've been wondering who the Wizard of g is. I was thinking that it would be someone who could lead with great vision, and I wonder if it miet be you."

"I'm flattered that you think so, but ideas are one thing and putting them into action is quite another," Ferret conceded.

"Raccoon suggested that value is the price someone would pay to purchase the company in the open market. I talked with Gander yesterday and he thawt that value was something to do with legitimate earnings." Rabbit laid out most of his case, hoping to entice Ferret to open up regarding his ideas.

"Raccoon's position is the most obvious, but Gander has it all wrong. Earnings are important, but it really comes down to whether or not the company is growing. That is the key."

"What do you mean?"

"I've been frustrated at the board meetings because we never talk about the future. We talk a lot about obtaining resources and production. We even talk about customers and our relative position in the marketplace. To me the real question is where we will be in ten years. The price of everything keeps going up and the market keeps expanding. We have to change each year to compensate for prices and expansion, but we don't spend enuf time discussing the long term."

"How do we do that?" Rabbit could see that Ferret was a reservoir behind a dam ready to burst forth with all his ideas. He just needed someone who would listen.

"Let me relate an experience," began Ferret.

The Nut Shop

Sometime ago I became aware of a Squirrel that ran a little shop selling walnuts and almonds. He became concerned about growth and began to analyze how revenue changed from year to year. In looking at sales, he found that he sold 100 pounds of walnuts at one dollar a pound for a total of $100. That same year he sold 50 pounds of almonds at two dollars a pound for a total of $100. So, total sales that year were $200.

He thawt it was interesting that he received the same revenue from each kind of nut, even thoe he sold twice the quantity of walnuts.

The next year, Squirrel worked very hard and when all was said and done, he had revenue of $242. He was curious to know what caused the 20 percent increase in sales, so he went back over his records. He found something very interesting.

He sold 110 pounds of walnuts at $1.10 per pound for a total of $121, and 55 pounds of almonds at $2.20 per pound for a total of $121. His volume had increased ten percent for each kind of nut. At the same time he had passed along cost increases so that he had a revenue rate increase of ten percent.

He understood why rates went up, but didn't quite know why there was an increase in the volume. After more investigation he found that: (1) Some of his old customers increased their demand; (2) New customers had been attracted away from a competing shop; and (3) Customers, who had never purchased nuts before became aware of his shop and started buying nuts from him.

He thawt he had everything figured out until the next year ended. Revenue was up another ten percent, but strange things were at work: (1) Rates were not increased at all; (2) The volume of walnut sales went down; (3) The volume of almond sales went up; and (4) He began selling cashews. This time, growth was not the result of a simple volume and rate increases, but rather revenue was the result of exchanging hier priced almonds for lower priced walnuts and the introduction of a new product, cashews."

As a result, he came to understand that—

Growth comes from Volume,
Exchange, Rates, and New Products

"Wow, I never thawt that growth could be so complex," Rabbit conceded.

"I think Red Maple Mill is quite adept at volume and rate increases, but exchange and new products---I'm not sure we are doing enuf there." Ferret seemed to be getting excited.

"I don't think we have ever talked about how exchange or the mix of products and new products can affect growth." Rabbit seemed puzzled.

"We haven't. Our business has always been a single product company that looks to growth as more of the same at hier prices. Sometimes you have to grow by changing, and that comes from effective Teamwork, Innovation, and Technology."

"What do you mean by that?" Rabbit asked.

Ferret outlined:

1. Teamwork brings people together to solve problems they couldn't do on their own.
2. Innovation is letting their minds explore wild ideas that often go beyond constraints.
3. Technology is employing the latest and best processes and mechanics that are available.

"Some companies embrace all of these, and many don't."

"How do you think our Company is doing?" Rabbit asked.

"We are lagging behind. The secret is to continually ask what the customer needs and not what are we able to do. I don't think we are keeping up at all in the area of exchange or new products. Do you know there is talk about using other materials than wood for shingles? Can you imagine what that would do to our plant? Maybe we are not really in the shingle business at all. Maybe we are really in the wood products business and need to rethink how we utilize the resources we have."

Rabbit was amazed. Ferret had a lot to say and yet seemed so quiet at the board meetings. "Why don't you bring this up at the meetings?"

"I've tried many times in the past, but everyone was so preoccupied with themselves and how they thawt Owl was ranking them that I didn't get much traction."

"Well, I'm impressed. You miet well be the Wizard of g. So to you, our value is based on the ever changing portfolio of our products as they affect growth."

"That's riet, our ability to expand into the future."

The conversation then trailed off into other areas as they enjoyed some liet refreshment. When Rabbit left he thanked Ferret for a wonderfully enlietning morning and wished him well. He wanted to go and see Porcupine next, but needed to contemplate what Ferret had said.

That evening Rabbit assessed the various positions. Raccoon thawt value was the price to sell the Company. Gander believed value a function of the Company's legitimate earnings. Ferret focused on how the company handles growth. Rabbit wondered where he had been all his life. Gander's remarks, about how companies change the numbers on their reports to make it look like they are doing well, were pause for concern. Ferret's comments about change and the possibility that wood shingles miet be replaced by another type of material were frietening. It was a much more dynamic world out there than Rabbit had ever imagined.

Thursday – June 4

The next day Rabbit was up early and attending to some chores around the house when he heard a knock at the door. Opening the door, he saw Skunk standing there. "I'm shocked that you are up so early," said Rabbit.

"I've got it!" declared an excited Skunk.

Rabbit had never seen Skunk so animated. She was drunk with enthusiasm. "You've got what?"

"I know how to value the company!"

Rabbit was taken aback. "You've figured it out?"

"Yes, it is so simple.

Skunk's Solution

Value is what someone will pay to buy all the assets.

If we were to liquidate the Red Maple Mill, what could we get if we sold the building, the land, the trees, the equipment, and the inventory?"

"Do we want to do that?"

"No, but that is how the value should be calculated," Skunk explained.

"Hmm, that is an interesting thawt," Rabbit mused. "I need to think about that a little bit."

"I just had to tell someone, but don't tell anyone else. I don't trust them."

"I'll keep it under my ears," promised Rabbit.

With that, Skunk turned and left.

Later that day Rabbit found Porcupine sitting on a log watching the stream roll by. "Do you mind if I sit a spell?" Rabbit asked.

"Be my guest," Porcupine welcomed. "I understand you've been visiting each of the board members and discussing the challenge. I suppose they have told you some of their theories."

"They've shared a few thawts with me, but I'm not sure I'm any closer to knowing what value is, or for that matter, who the next Wizard of g miet be. We have some very talented members on our board, and as far as I'm concerned it could be any one of them."

"I suppose you want to hear my theories?" Porcupine posed.

"Not if you don't want to," Rabbit responded.

"I don't mind. I've watched the world a long time--all the comings and goings--and it seems to me, it's a function of doing what you say you'll do."

"What do mean by that?" Rabbit questioned.

"Let me tell you a story about a Pack-Rat and his moving and storage business:

Moving and Storage

A Pack-Rat decided to start a moving and storage business. He thawt this would provide full employment for other Pack-Rats in his community. There appeared to be a lot of demand in the area so it seemed a good idea.

He took his own savings to pay for a sign to advertise his service, and he placed it on one of the main roads. His first job was for Chipmunk, whom he had known for years, who needed help moving to a new home. Because of Pack-Rat's reputation for fair dealing, Chipmunk had no problem inviting him to do the job. Pack-Rat had little trouble handling that first job on his own with the resources he had, and word soon spread about his service.

He was next contacted by a group of Quail that needed to move a large quantity of seed from a field to a thicket. They asked if Pack-Rat could store part of the seed for several months. After assessing the job he decided he needed to employ several workers and hire a storage facility. The workers agreed to pledge their time and resources to get the job done. The storage facility, however, wanted some guarantee the business would continue into the future and have sufficient earnings to make ongoing payments before they would agree to cooperate.

Pack-Rat began to wonder if he had bid the job hie enuf to cover all costs and provide an adequate return for his own time and assets. He began to think about risk: the risk of not having enuf workers and space to fulfill his promises; the risk of revenue enuf to pay for wages and rent; the risk of generating an adequate profit to pursue more jobs; and the risk that his business would continue with enuf clients to make payments.

Risk was having enuf resources to do what he had committed to.

"I didn't know risk was so important," Rabbit noted.

"It is critical. If you review this tale you will see that five elements were in play:

Conditions: There appeared to be demand.
Capital: He took his own savings to pay.
Character: A reputation for fair dealing.
Collateral: A pledge of time and resources.
Capacity: A guarantee of payment.

"I see what you mean," Rabbit noted.

"Each one of these provides a measure of risk. If they are all positively provided for, then the business has great value. If any of them is compromised, the result is increased risk and a lower value for the company."

"That is an amazing analysis," Rabbit conceded.

"It can be a vicious cycle for many companies. They need resources to fulfill their commitments, but in order to fulfill their commitments, they need resources," Porcupine instructed.

"That certainly is a difficult problem. You can't sell because you don't have the financing, and you can't get the financing because you don't have the sales. Kind of a chicken and egg problem," Rabbit observed.

"It's a hard nut to crack. It is not only having enuf resources, but an "adequate margin of error" pad to handle fluctuations from time to time. The risk of not keeping your word is the ultimate risk and the determinate of value."

"So it sounds like having available resources is the most critical thing. I'm gaining more and more respect for the wisdom of the members of the board. I'm beginning to wonder why I'm even on the board and what I have to contribute," Rabbit wondered.

"Don't be hard on yourself. I've watched you in action and you have a wonderful capacity for listening, communication and teamwork. I'm glad you're one of us," Porcupine reassured.

"Do you mind if I ask you to clarify one point?"

"Go riet ahead."

"You said that when there is increased risk the value would be lower. What do you mean by that?"

"Take for example the market. If I was reasonably sure that the demand for shingles would continue uninterrupted well into the future, then I would be quite satisfied with an average earnings number. On the other hand, if there was some concern that the market miet change in such a way that the future was in doubt, then I would want my current earnings to be hier. Everyone wants safety, and they are willing to accept lower profits in return for the security; but if things are uncertain, they need a little hier comfort zone that could be reflected in stronger earnings."

"How does that translate to value?" Rabbit inquired.

"If earnings were fixed at $1, and risk was low then I could expect the company to be worth more because that dollar would be pretty predictable. On the other hand, if risk was hie, then I would be more uncertain that level of earnings would continue into the future and so the value would be low. There is a direct relationship between returns, value, and risk," Porcupine explained.

They continued visiting for some time and finally Rabbit excused himself. "It's been a pleasure visiting with you. I've learned a lot, thank you."

That niet Rabbit took inventory again. He decided to reject the arguments of Raccoon and Skunk. The price someone would pay to take over the operations of the company, as Raccoon suggested, was one thing, and the value to the stakeholders was probably something else.

Also, the price of selling off the assets, as Skunk had suggested, did not seem to reflect the value either. Then, he cawt himself: Maybe he was dismissing them too easily. Skunk and Raccoon were his closest friends and maybe the old cliché that familiarity breeds contempt was true. He paused for a moment, but only a moment. No, he was being rational and those two options didn't seem to make sense to him. Red Maple Mill wasn't for sale and he didn't think it was about to be liquidated. Value had to be something else, if it was to represent a venture that would continue into the future.

Then there were the issues that Gander, Ferret, and Porcupine had suggested. Gander said it was based on earnings, Ferret said it was based on growth, and Porcupine said it was a function of risk. Each had a very compelling argument and each seemed to have thawt it thrue very well. One of them had to be the Wizard of g, but which one?

Rabbit determined to make his last investigative inquiry the next day. He would visit with Fox. Rabbit felt intimidated by Fox, who always seemed to have a lot of data and applied models to everything. He was smart and could eat you alive in almost any argument. Rabbit would need to be cautious.

Friday – June 5

Rabbit approached Fox's home and gently knocked on the door. After what seemed an eternity, the door slowly opened. Fox was standing there looking down thrue glasses that hung low on his nose. "I've been expecting you," Fox precisely stated an authoritative muse. "Come in."

The two proceeded into the main living area that seemed more like a study than a place for entertaining. There was a massive bookcase that covered all of one wall and a large table in the middle of the room with a lamp in the center. The liet of the lamp illuminated the mass of books and papers spread over the table. "I understand you've been doing the rounds? So have I," Fox announced. "Perhaps we can compare notes."

Rabbit knew he was going to have to offer up most of what he had learned and hoped that Fox would share something with him. He held nothing back and laid everything on the table. As he revealed all that he had learned, he observed that Fox was quietly taking it all in. He sat back with his chin on his chest, arms folded across his belly, eyes peering over his low riding glasses.

When Rabbit finished, Fox asked, "What is your conclusion? Who is the wizard of g?"

"I don't think it is Raccoon or Skunk, but I could be wrong. It miet be Gander, Ferret, or Porcupine. Or it could be you," Rabbit offered reverently.

"I suppose Owl will not only want an accurate calculation of what the value of the Company is, but some sense of endorsement from the members of the board. For that reason I'm compelled to share with you some of my thawts. I think that earnings, growth, and risk are all components of what makes value, but they have to be combined into the correct calculation. I've been studying these matters for a long time and reviewed much of the authoritative literature. I would have to say that I'm in complete agreement with the experts," Fox announced.

Rabbit felt like a novice coming to the oracle. He sat in complete admiration and listened to each word as it fell from Fox's mouth. Fox stood up and walked over to a large board that hung on the wall next to the bookcase. Rabbit followed and planted in a chair next to the table in front of the board. Fox then began a period of instruction where he diagramed long equations and sophisticated calculations on the board. He quoted extensively from renowned authorities as he filled the board with numbers and Greek symbols.

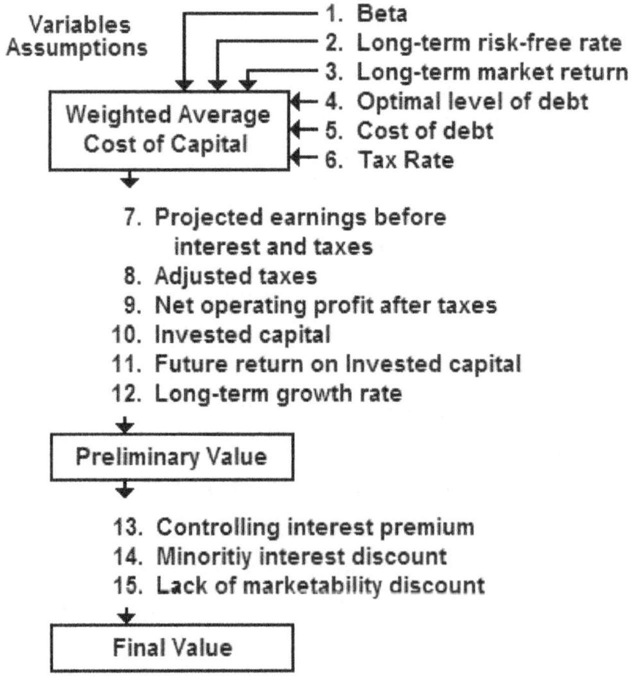

derive value. E or earnings are divided by 0.01 times G (or growth) to the power of minus five R (or risk) plus five. All of this is equal to the value of whatever is being measured.

Since this simple model was discovered, it has made determining value much easier and more precise than more complex approaches. The only challenge is coming up with the correct measurers of earnings, growth, and risk. Great care needs to be given in selecting the best assumptions for to be applied to the formula.

The model has been tested to calculate the price of each of the 30 Dow Jones Industrial Stocks against other valuation tools for a particular period. The results from the Residual Income Model and Discounted Cash Flow Model were both compared the results generated by the Capitalized Earnings Model. The price generated by each model was compared to the actual price of the stock for each company. It was found that all of the models were fairly comparable and gave relatively good results. The difference was that the Capitalized Earnings Model was much easier to apply.

Earnings

The first step is to project earnings or the net income for the next year. This can be somewhat difficult, but the assumption is made that a company will generate a fairly consistent percentage of revenue that will flow to the bottom line over time. This will smooth out the volatility that occurs from year to year. Therefore, add up the net income for the past five years and dividing it by the revenue for the same time frame. Suppose a company's average net income is 8.5% of revenue.

We are trying to find normalized earnings. It is easier to project revenue than earnings. Net Income is a number that is the result of thousands of transactions, estimates, and adjustments. The average for five years has a tendency to smooth out all the adjustments and volatility. This past year revenue grew by 10% and a company's marketing department has predicted that next year's volume will be up another 10%. Budgeting anticipates revenue will be $1,500 million in the coming year.

Now multiply $1,500 million by 8.5% and find a predicted $127.50 million in normalized earnings. That's the earnings. If there are some specific changes in the overall expenses of the company in the future, then an adjustment to this number miet be incorporated. The next challenge is to determine a number to use for growth?

Growth

The next step is to project the next three to five years growth rate. The question becomes whether that is for revenue, cash flow, dividends, or earnings?

It should be earnings, but since they can be very volatile a lot of analysts look at a more strategic growth rate in revenue. This could be discussed at length, but more analysts prefer to use the growth in revenue. Growth was 10% this past year, but with downward and descended toward the group. Finally, Owl touched down and was in their midst.

His head swiveled in its usual manner, surveying each member of the board. He paused for a split second when his eyes rested on Rabbit, who was brimming with confidence and pride. Then Owl spoke: "We will begin--" he paused and nodded at Raccoon, who was standing to Rabbit's left--"with Raccoon, and then continue around in a clockwise manner."

Rabbit instantly realized that he would be last. He was glad of that. "I want each of you to step forward and offer your answer to the question I posed last week. What is the value of Red Maple Mill? Remember, more than just a number, I want an explanation and justification." Owl looked strate at Rabbit for a second, and then glancing away he said, "Raccoon, you may now begin."

As unusually brief as the last meeting had been, this meeting promised to be unusually long. Each member in turn stepped forward, announced a number for the value, and explained their reasoning. All were substantially the same discussions they had shared with Rabbit during the week. Some were more polished and added a few bells and whistles, but the substance was the same. Skunk was standing to Rabbit's riet and offered his solution just before Rabbit's turn. When he explained the value was based on selling off the assets of the company, there was a noticeable gasp from the board members. It was the only audible sound from the board members during the presentations up to that point.

Finally, it was Rabbit's turn. "Before I begin, I'd like to thank the other members of the board for helping me understand the concept of value. I have spent the past week visiting with each of you and I tried to glean as much information as I could. You have all been very helpful and I have great respect for your individual talents. I want to thank you."

"It is my opinion the value of Red Maple Mill is," and then Rabbit expressed a figure. The other figures that had been previously presented covered a broad range which Rabbit's fell easily within. "I feel this is the correct number. Let me explain."

"I learned a great deal from Fox, who helped me realized the expression of a value should be the result of a definable calculation. I could never hope to master the elaborate and elegant steps that he went thrue to arrive at his number. My formula is much simpler and helped me frame the basic relationships as I saw them."

"I agree with Skunk that if we were to close Red Maple Mill, the value would be what we could generate by selling the assets, but I feel Red Maple Mill has a future and should be continued. Likewise, Raccoon's value, based on the price another entity would pay to acquire Red Maple Mill, may be correct, but I'm not advocating that we go into open negotiations to determine what that price miet be."

"That leaves me with the three factors that were proposed by Gander, Ferret, and Porcupine:

Earnings, Growth, and Risk. I think these are critical elements, and I want to give these individuals full credit for the input they gave me in helping me to identify the approach I've selected."

"After extensive research I found a method that is called "The Bunker Curve." It is a capitalization rate model, which means that a factor is divided into normalized earnings to arrive at value. The factor is derived from the long-term growth rate adjusted for risk. It is based on a best-guess regarding not only the current state of affairs, but what the future will be.

"I want to thank Ferret for opening my eyes to the power of growth. This has become the foundation of my whole formula." Rabbit gave a thankful nod to Ferret.

"I begin with our projected Company earnings for next year. I want to make sure the number is clean and free from manipulation. I also want to use it as a representation of what the future will be. If we had an unusually profitable year, then I miet adjust next year's projection downward a bit to reflect a more normal anticipated trend. If this year was unusually weak, I would adjust the projection upward."

"But next year's projected earnings are only the beginning. Next I want to examine projected growth, not just short-term growth, but an average of short-term and long-term. This is a very delicate decision and involves an assessment of several things: Red Maple Mill's marketing efforts, the strength of our products in the market place, and our ability and willingness to innovate and change."

"We need a greater effort in the areas that Ferret defined: Teamwork, Innovation, and Technology. My assessment is that we are not doing very well riet now in those areas, so my formula reflects a modest growth projection for the future."

"The last factor to incorporate is risk. Porcupine has certainly demonstrated the importance of risk, and that is primarily why 'The Bunker Curve' appealed to me. It was unclear to me just how to assess risk until I thawt about those who are paid to do just that. I know Otter, our Company financial officer, has continually told us the bank, who lends us money, is constantly evaluating risk and setting our interest rate up or down based on not only the general economy, but on their assessment of our own probability for success or default."

"In most of the literature that I read, growth serves as a fair multiple when interest rates are hier. When rates are lower; the simple approach no longer works."

"The three numbers: earnings, growth and risk, are utilized in the formula to calculate value. I spent long hours testing the model against all the data that I could gather and feel very comfortable the result is a good number. The Bunker Curve formula is:

$$\mathbf{V = E / [.01g^{-(5r+.5)}]}$$

E represents next year's normalized earnings; g is the average long-term growth rate; and r is the risk adjusted interest rate. This sounds complex, but I have a chart that shows various combinations of risk adjusted interest rates and average long-term growth rates."

At this point Rabbit produced a chart and placed it in front of the shingle that was resting on a log next to him. "This chart is the result of applying the formula to various average long-term growth rates and average adjusted interest rates. You can see for each growth rate there is a column, and for each interest rate there is a row. All you need to do is find the intersection of the two to find the number to be divided into earnings."

"My assumption is that the Average Long-term growth rate for the Company will be 6% and that our Risk adjusted interest rate will be 8%. From the chart I find the intersection of those two assumptions to be 12.6%. I divided that number into next year's earnings and the result is the value of the company"

The Bunker Curve:
"Value is determined by the interaction of Earnings, Growth, and Risk."

At the conclusion of Rabbit's presentation, he quietly stepped back into his place with the others. Owl swiveled his head around, surveying the board and then said: "I want to thank all of you for the work you have done. I know each of you are attached to your own methodology, but let me ask a simple question---If you had to chose someone other than yourself to be the next CEO, who would it be?"

They looked at each other, trying to think of who they miet pick. Then Owl added, "I would also ask you to consider who has been most diligent in soliciting input, been open to new ideas, and tried to pull you all together? I agree with Ferret's assessment that growth is the most important thing. That is why I referred to the next CEO as the Wizard of g, but growth can't happen in isolation. It is now up to you, as a board, to determine who the next leader will be."

A secret ballot was held and a hat was passed around for all to place their ballots in. When everyone was finished, Owl slowly pulled the final ballot and announced, "It appears that I've just pulled Rabbit out of the hat." Owl turned to Rabbit and invited him to come and stand beside him at the Gnarly Oak.

Quest for Knowledge

(The fable continues)

Owl turned to Rabbit and welcomed him as the new leader and Chairman of the Board. As Rabbit climbed up to the limb where Owl was perched, he looked around to see the reaction from the various board members. He could sense that change was not going to be easy and knew he had to do something immediately to move the transition forward.

"If I miet say something," Rabbit blurted out. All of the board members looked at him. "I think it is only riet that we celebrate the wonderful work that Owl has done by giving him this moment of recognition and respect."

The timing had been just riet and in focusing on Owl, it diverted attention from Rabbit. All of the board members shouted hurray---hurray---hurray as Owl extended his wings to quiet the group.

"It has been a pleasure to serve. I think our efforts have made a significant difference and I think we all can take some pride in what has been accomplished. I recognize that change is never easy and I want all of you to give Rabbit your full support as you try to move Red Maple Mill forward. He will have a great deal of growing to do and needs each one of you to support him." Owl said.

He continued. "I recognize that times are changing and it is a good time for dynamic leadership: New ideas and a new vision. This is a wonderful venture that has served its customers well, but I can see dark clouds on the horizon. It is time for all of you to come together. That is one reason I'm pleased with your decision. Rabbit has demonstrated a willingness to work with each of you. I know he will continue to listen and Red Maple Mill is in good hands. If there is nothing further, we shall end the board meeting. Thank You."

As the board members turned to leave, Rabbit looked at Owl and asked: "Do you have a moment that I miet speak with you alone?"

"Certainly," Owl responded.

"You have been a wonderful leader and I have enjoyed being a good follower. I don't know if I'm up to the task of leading this organization," Rabbit admitted.

"I can understand your concern. That is only natural, but let me assure you that if you continue to do what you have done this past week, you will be successful. Leadership comes from reaching out, listening, and taking decisive action."

"You had a challenge and what did you do? You sawt answers thrue information, discussion, and study. Then upon reflection you tried to make sense of what you knew and how it applied. When you finally arrived at what was the best conclusion you went forward boldly. What you must do now, is to continue as you have done. Be humble and listen. When the answer comes---then be decisive. I liked the way you presented your conclusion: with confidence."

look like it should be grouped in an industry, but in reality it is culturally more closely related to a completely different business because of shared ancestry."

Hedgehog just shook his head. "I suppose you could say it that way. Speaking of ancestry, there is the concept of evolution and that thrue natural selection some things become more common, while others become less common over time.

"Certainly, survival of the fittest is inherent in commerce. Those businesses that adapt to their environment will continue to survive and those that don't won't. Yes, I think that applies also. Please go on, this is getting good. What about growth?" Rabbit pressed.

"Growth is affected by genetic factors, as well as environmental conditions: an adequate supply of water and diet; and specifically for plants: appropriate liet, space, and temperature. Most organisms have the potential for growth if they are allowed to," Hedgehog instructed.

"I think genetic factors or culture, resources and the environment are also fundamental for growth in any business. Organically speaking, I would summarize the various points as:

1. Earnings are the result of energy and exchange:
2. Risk derives from environmental culling where the strongest businesses survive and the weak fail.

3. Growth results from the synergy of energy and exchange; a supportive culture; and adapting to environmental conditions."

"You mention synergy. I think you have inadvertently revealed another living principle. Every living thing interacts with other organisms and its environment. One reason that biological systems can be difficult to study is that so many different interactions with other organisms and the environment are possible, even on the smallest of scales. Can you tell me why growth is so important to you?" Hedgehog asked.

"I have developed a theory of how to value a business that has growth as its central theme. Let me show you, in very simple terms." Rabbit scratched the following diagram on in the dirt:

VALUE TRIANGLE

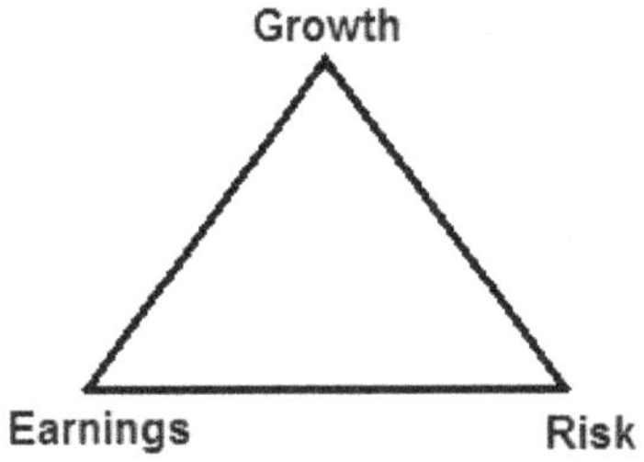

"Miet I suggest that your approach is organic," Hedgehog offered.

"What do you mean?" Rabbit wanted to know.

"I think if it is growth based, then it is organic."

"That seems to make sense," Rabbit agreed.

"As you yourself have just said: Growth results from the synergy of energy and exchange; a supportive culture; and adapting to environmental conditions," Hedgehog observed. "What did you say was the result of your model?"

"Value, and I think value is determined by the interaction of growth, earnings, and risk. Most financial models have a tendency to manipulate a lot of numbers and don't pay enuf attention to the living part of the business. I don't think you can correctly predict growth, earnings, and risk unless you investigate and understand the organic nature of a company," Rabbit explained.

"I think I understand," Hedgehog nodded.

"Is this garden your business? What I mean to ask is do you make your living thue this garden?" Rabbit asked.

"Yes I do. I sell plants and seeds to a broad range of customers," Hedgehog responded. "Perhaps you could value my business with your model."

"That is a very interesting idea. First we would have to predict what your earnings are going to be next year," Rabbit instructed.

"My revenue has grown by 20% every year for the past five years and I would expect it to be the same for next year. From that it is very easy to predict my earnings."

"That is a pretty aggressive growth rate. There is a general rule that suggests:

Eventually, all growth rates move to the average of the economy.

If the economy is growing at a combined real growth plus inflation of 6%, then eventually almost all companies will move toward that. If I were going to put a growth rate in the model for you, I'd balance it half for your short-term growth of 20% and half for the long-term economy of 6%. The average would be 13% and that is what I would use," Rabbit said.

"I guess that is reasonable."

"If a company grew at 20% per year for the next fifty years, it would increase by 9,100%. That is just not possible. What risk adjusted interest rate do you have to pay to get funding?" Rabbit offered.

Hedgehog responded and Rabbit calculated the value of the business, incorporating the next year's earnings, a 13% growth rate, and the interest rate. "That is close to what I would have expected it to be worth," Hedgehog noted.

They continued a very enjoyable dialogue when Rabbit inquired: "Excuse me, could you tell me if I'm on the riet road to find Big Dog?"

"I don't know about that, but I do have a map I could let you look at." Hedgehog went into his cottage and appeared shortly carrying a large rolled paper.

Hedgehog spread the map be
pointed to the Meadow at the far
"Perhaps that's where you'll find

Rabbit surveyed the map exte
commit it to memory. Then he tha
his hospitality and the wonderful
He said that he had to be pressing
bidding farewell, continued on his

After some travel thrue a forest,
clearing with a pond. There at the e
was Mother Duck and her little duck
busily trying to keep them all togeth

Rabbit could not resist asking ho
The response he received was not wh
"I almost wonder if it is more than I
trying to keep all these little ones tog
danger, and growing as they should."

"What do you mean?" Rabbit inqu
as if you are doing a fine job.

"Raising little ones is a challenge.
inquisitive and adventurous. It seems li
I've reached a state of comfort and equ
everything changes. They are growing
pushing the boundaries of their world. I
staircase of stability for a few days and
suddenly they get creative and we are in
can establish a time of stability again."

"Wow, I never thawt of it like that: I
it is a difficult task. Are the periods of ch

dictable so that you know when they are ming?" Rabbit inquired.

"That's the other problem; you never know when will happen. I've finally decided it is impossible to ve absolute control over them, I just need to epherd them along and do the best I can to keep em out of danger. As long as I accept change and ncourage them to grow in a reasonable way, I feel at I'm controlling the general direction, but not dividual development."

"So these periods of change are pretty random?"

"Well, actually there is a balance. I intentionally ush them forward and teach them many things in a ather formal way and change happens, but on other ccasions they spontaneously do things that I can't nticipate," Mother Duck admitted.

Rabbit pressed the point: "Let me see if I understand. Between periods of stability are occasions of controlled change as the result of teaching new things, or change that is uncontrolled coming from naturally responding to the environment."

"I suppose you could say it like that. Let me offer one other observation: There are many external forces that act on them, such as my teaching moments, but they do not change until they have internalized or accepted the new and broader vision."

"Growth comes in steps as change is internalized."

Hedgehog spread the map before Rabbit and pointed to the Meadow at the far left of the map. "Perhaps that's where you'll find Big Dog."

Rabbit surveyed the map extensively and tried to commit it to memory. Then he thanked Hedgehog for his hospitality and the wonderful exchange of ideas. He said that he had to be pressing forward and bidding farewell, continued on his way.

After some travel thrue a forest, Rabbit came to a clearing with a pond. There at the edge of the pond was Mother Duck and her little ducklings. She was busily trying to keep them all together in her charge.

Rabbit could not resist asking how she was doing. The response he received was not what he expected. "I almost wonder if it is more than I can handle, trying to keep all these little ones together, out of danger, and growing as they should."

"What do you mean?" Rabbit inquired. "It looks as if you are doing a fine job.

"Raising little ones is a challenge. They are all so inquisitive and adventurous. It seems like just when I've reached a state of comfort and equilibrium, everything changes. They are growing constantly and pushing the boundaries of their world. It is like a staircase of stability for a few days and then suddenly they get creative and we are in chaos until I can establish a time of stability again."

"Wow, I never thawt of it like that: I can see that it is a difficult task. Are the periods of chaos pretty predictable so that you know when they are coming?" Rabbit inquired.

"That's the other problem; you never know when it will happen. I've finally decided it is impossible to have absolute control over them, I just need to shepherd them along and do the best I can to keep them out of danger. As long as I accept change and encourage them to grow in a reasonable way, I feel that I'm controlling the general direction, but not individual development."

"So these periods of change are pretty random?"

"Well, actually there is a balance. I intentionally push them forward and teach them many things in a rather formal way and change happens, but on other occasions they spontaneously do things that I can't anticipate," Mother Duck admitted.

Rabbit pressed the point: "Let me see if I understand. Between periods of stability are occasions of controlled change as the result of teaching new things, or change that is uncontrolled coming from naturally responding to the environment."

"I suppose you could say it like that. Let me offer one other observation: There are many external forces that act on them, such as my teaching moments, but they do not change until they have internalized or accepted the new and broader vision."

"Growth comes in steps as change is internalized."

“Thank you for sharing some personal thawts with me. I’ve found them to be very instructive,” Rabbit said with gratitude.

As Mother Duck and her charges moved away across the pond, Rabbit began to reflect on what he had heard. It seemed there could be fundamental truths that were applicable to a company. Growth seemed to be disruptive, just like the staircase Mother Duck had referred to.

STABILITY-CHANGE STAIRCASE

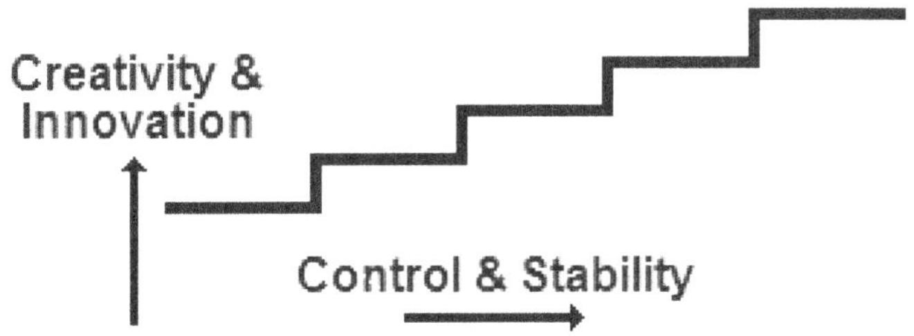

Rabbit thawt of it as a Stability-Change Staircase. Could it be that the whole growth process was like that. Does one have to give up absolute power in order for the organization to move forward? Rabbit also wondered if this balance between formal and fluid change was the same with a company. In addition, true cultural change is never complete until the organization internalizes it.

Rabbit continued his journey, but could not help reflecting on what Mother Duck had said. That niet he felt the day had been particularly instructive.

Tuesday – June 9

The next morning Rabbit started off with renewed excitement. He felt that he was already starting to learn things and gain a little magic. As he proceeded down the road, he noticed that the surrounding trees and vegetation became much thicker. The road narrowed and became a slice between towering trees. Because of the denseness of the forest the liet was restricted and it almost appeared as evening, thoe it was mid-morning.

After a slow gradual bend in the road it straitened out for about a mile. As he moved along another thing struck him as odd: there was not a sound. He stopped for a moment to listen and that is when he cawt siet of four large black ravens that seemed to have come out of no-where and were sitting on the road in front of him.

As he watched, one of them sprung into the air, swooped over his head and landed some distance behind him. It was then that he realized that he miet be in danger. His path to the front was blocked by the Ravens and now his exit to the rear was closed. The sides of the road were virtual walls of almost impenetrable webs of branches, leaves, and foliage.

He tried to collect his composure, when two of the Ravens leaped into the air and flew strate at him.

"I'm in the business of helping people. I find that to be extremely rewarding," Chipmunk said.

"The business of helping people: How is that a business?" Rabbit puzzled.

"Even non-profits, such as my own little venture, must adhere to business concepts. I would never violate the seven sins of business."

"The what?" Rabbit recoiled.

"The seven sins of business," Chipmunk affirmed.

"What are you talking about?" Rabbit pressed.

Chipmunk lead Rabbit thrue the forest to a little cottage where he lived.

"There they are," Chipmunk pointed.

1. Leadership without Vision
2. Cost without Benefit
3. Work without Skill
4. Resources without Controls
5. Process without Improvement
6. Competition without Advantage
7. Opportunity without Pursuit

Rabbit studied the chart for a while and then said: "Well, I can't criticize them, but how on earth do they apply to a non-profit venture?"

"You have to have a vision and know what you're doing. You also have to put effort into those things that will bring you the greatest reward, whether financial or otherwise. It all makes sense. I love helping others and since my basic needs are taken care of, I work for the greater good, as I see it," Chipmunk said.

He continued: "A non-profit is like any other business with two exceptions: (1) There is no equity, per se, and so there are no owners that must receive a financial return on their investment; and (2) The revenue the business receives may be subsidized by interested parties. The community that benefits from the non-profit puts up the funding to acquire assets and contributes to ongoing operational costs. Other than that the non-profit is like any other business. It must grow to keep up with inflation and market share, which is financed either from the community that supports it or by generating earnings to support that growth. If the community's financial support is limited then there must be earnings for growth in addition to borrowing for short-term financial needs." Chipmunk explained.

"So then a lot of the seven sins of business would apply," Rabbit mused.

"That's riet."

"I wonder if my valuation model would work," Rabbit pondered out loud.

"If it applies to regular business, I think it miet," Chipmunk interjected.

"I would need an estimate of next year's earnings, the rate of growth, and the risk adjusted interest rate on borrowed funds," Rabbit stated.

"The limitation would be the extent to which earnings were offset by community support. That should have to be factored in. We could always estimate what earnings would need to be to sustain the target growth."

"That is a lot to think about. I will have to ponder it for a while and then maybe do some testing to see if the model would work. Of course the product of the model is the value of the business in terms of dollars and since no one is interested in purchasing the business, I guess it doesn't make much sense anyway," Rabbit concluded.

"Not so fast. I think there may be some reasons to calculate the number, even thoe what you say is true. A community miet like to see that number and then add to it the non-financial value they derive, as they see it. Both numbers could be important," Chipmunk concluded.

Rabbit was in deep reflection when Chipmunk continued: "I don't think you'd better return to the road at this point. If you follow me, I can show you where the forest breaks and the road is visible again."

"That would be great," said Rabbit. They left the cottage and Rabbit followed Chipmunk along a narrow path that trailed back and forth along the forest floor. Finally, they came to the last trees before a broad expanse of grass.

"This is as far as I go," Chipmunk indicated.

"I really don't know how to thank you."

"It's been my pleasure. I love to thwart those evil Ravens. It is more excitement than you could buy at an amusement park."

“Thanks again,” Rabbit offered and worked his way thrue the grass to where the road was. At the road he looked back toward the forest to see if there was any sign of the Ravens, but there was nothing.

He sat down at the side of the road and began to take stock of the damage. He had several scratches and cuts, but nothing that wouldn’t heal. Thinking to himself, he wondered if he hadn’t just climbed a rung on his personal staircase. It had seemed pretty stable up until then. He rolled over and over in his mind what had happened and if he had learned anything from the experience.

After resting for a bit, he continued down the road in the direction of Big Dog. Before long, he came to a Bloodhound sitting by the side of the road. The Bloodhound appeared troubled. “Excuse me, but could you give me some direction?” Rabbit inquired.

“Oh hello, what do you need?”

“I was wondering if this is the way to where I miet find Big Dog?” Rabbit asked.

Turning and looking down the road Bloodhound responded: “Yea, continue in the direction you are going.”

“Miet I ask you another question?” Rabbit issued.

“What is that?”

“Is there something bothering you?”

“I’m worried about my company. We are at a crossroads and I need to make some hard decisions, but I’m not sure what to do.” Bloodhound relied.

"Maybe it would help if you just talked about it. I've got big ears," Rabbit said with a smile.

"Well, I'm in the retail business and I've got a chain of five stores in five towns within a region. I developed a formula where each store is managed by a part owner and I stress an aggressive customer orientation. Each store does well, but I think we could expand the chain infinitely by replicating the formula in hundreds of other places."

"I don't see any problem there. As a matter of fact that seems like an excellent growth model," Rabbit noted.

"It would be except the world is changing. As I look for additional financing to expand, my bankers are pressing me to find ways to make each store more profitable. I tried to centralize some functions, but they have failed miserably. Those experiences have tapped some of my resources and only made things worse. I need to show my bankers that I've got a model for growth they can understand. They want order and structure."

"Do you have any ideas?" Rabbit encouraged.

"I've come up with what I call the Change of Direction Elbow or CODE." Bloodhound produced a paper and laid it on the ground.

"That looks really complicated, but impressive. Do you mind if I ask a few questions?"

"Go riet ahead." Bloodhound said.

"What is the Network of Economic Ties?"

"That is basically the external environment that is defined by the company's market area. It is a grid of stability with intersecting networks of products and services. I call it my Network of Economic Ties or NET, because it is the market environment I focus on."

"What is the Opportunity Hole in the middle?"

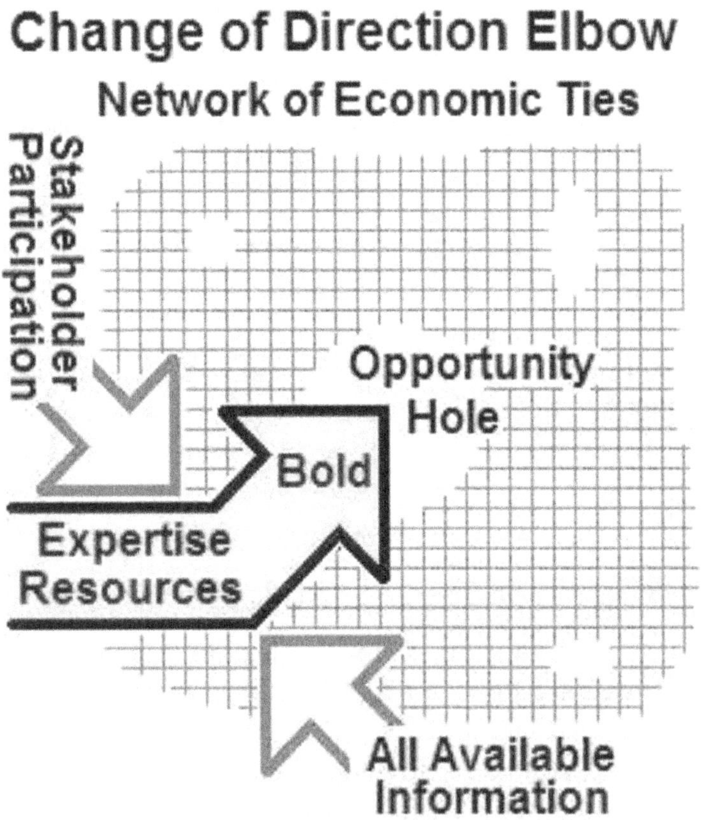

"The Network is never stable. It is constantly changing as people's tastes, wants, and needs evolve with new ideas and technologies. Thrue this evolution, holes of opportunity open up in the grid. They are underserved areas waiting for someone to fill the void."

"That is fascinating. I'm beginning to wonder why you're worried. You seem to have worked the whole thing out."

"Not quite. You see this arrow that I've labeled as 'Expertise and Resources'?"

"Yes," Rabbit found it on the chart.

"Most companies find a comfortable path that seems to be successful and take their place as a part of the overall NET. The problem arises when companies change direction to take advantage of 'Opportunity Holes'. Unfortunately, continuing on the same old path is usually limiting and eventually runs out of potential."

"Changing directions usually takes some kind of innovative adjustment in the company. If you identify the opportunity early, a flex in the new direction for the company is small, like bending your elbow just a little. But the longer you wait to take advantage of the change the sharper the bend and the more traumatic for the company."

"In what ways is it traumatic?" Rabbit asked.

"As the company changes some existing expertise and resources are no longer needed and new ideas and talents must be cultivated and developed. This leads to turnover of employees, which is usually hardest on the more senior workforce. There is almost a proportional relationship between the amount of change and the stress it places on employees with years of experience."

"So, the longer at the company the harder it is to change. Is that riet?" Rabbit suggested.

"That's correct, but when you lose valuable senior workers, you also compromise the company's ability to generate revenue. The paradox is that as you try to change to pursue opportunities, you are also in danger of crippling the company's ability to succeed."

"I notice that you have the word 'Bold' at the end of the arrow. What is that all about?"

"When you know you're going to have to change, you must aggressively move with boldness. The timid fail," Bloodhound responded. "You have to...

sniff out new opportunities and begin the change early."

"This is brilliant. Don't your bankers like this?" Rabbit wanted to know.

"I haven't shown it to them yet. It really isn't complete. I've got two other arrows directed at Expertise and Resources to show that you need all available information and stakeholder participation to make the best decision."

"I still don't get it, you seem to have put all the pieces together. Your banks are going to love it," Rabbit puzzled.

"You can change and find a new direction, but the problem is profitability and risk. Will the

Opportunity Hole generate strong earnings? Everyone does something and provides service to someone. You must be selective and identify those services that will be of such value that the customer is willing to pay the price for them. Valued Customer Service is usually the result of a specialized talent, procedure, product, or market. Then you must protect your special niche. It isn't the case of just doing something, but doing the riet thing."

"The risk of change is also extremely hie. Bankers don't like risk, particularly if there is employee turnover and instability of workforce. They want sufficient assurance that success will follow before they even consider extending financial support. That is why protecting your niche is so important."

"Do you mind if I show you something?" Rabbit asked.

"No go riet ahead," Bloodhound encouraged.

"I've got a model of my own that I'm working on. It is how I proposed to set the value of a company." Rabbit produced a paper that revealed a diagram. He presented it to Bloodhound.

"You've just mentioned Earnings, Growth, and Risk. That is exactly what my model takes into consideration when calculating value," Rabbit said excitedly. "I think the most critical thing is growth and you have shown me a wonderful way to look at growth."

VALUE TRIANGLE

"You have a great model there. Growth is certainly the key to increasing value, but it has to be within the constraints of earnings and risk. As I just mentioned, I have most recently failed at my attempt to introduce centralized functions for my company. I took the risk and now earnings will be off. Not only that, but the bankers are pulling back, which will limit expansion, and overall growth."

"Do you have any idea what went wrong?"

"I think it was in the area of stakeholder participation. I didn't bring my store managers into the loop early in the process and they didn't support the change."

"Couldn't they see the benefits?"

"Managing people is a delicate thing. The process has to be a balance of top-down and bottom-up. I guess it could also be that my vision of what the change should be was not on target."

"Let me ask you a question. How much of change should be fluid versus formal. Everyone gets ideas and a fluid process allows input from all stakeholders. A formal process is more directed. I would say fluid is bottom-up and formal is top-down."

"I think you're riet. Whatever the case I've got to go back to the drawing board and find a way to make this work."

"This has been an extremely instructive exchange. I want to thank you for sharing your ideas. Whether you know it or not, you have helped me."

"I suppose that telling someone has helped me to focus just where my problem miet be," Bloodhound admitted.

"Tell me what you estimate to be next year's normalized earnings; your short-term growth; and the risk adjusted interest rate your bankers are charging you for borrowing," Rabbit instructed.

Bloodhound gave his best estimate of each and Rabbit went to work calculating the value of the company. "There is what I think your company is worth," Rabbit said. "It would be easy for you to play what-if now and change one of the variables at a time and see how it would change the overall value."

Rabbit adjusted the numbers to show that even if earnings were low, as growth increased value went up and as the interest rate went up the value decreased. "It's kind of a fun way to see what the possibilities are," Rabbit said.

"Fascinating, I think I can use this with my bankers," Bloodhound seemed thankful.

"I need to be on my way. I do hope you work it out. As far as I can see you will get there," Rabbit encouraged as he turned and left.

Rabbit traveled for some time and then, being worn out from the stress of the day relaxed for the niet. He thawt about the incidents with the Ravens, the Chipmunk, and the Bloodhound and wondered what he had learned. Suddenly, he began to see some correlations.

He reflected: "I was traveling along the same old road as many companies do when my way was impeded. I found myself in a network of economic ties or the place where my road carried me. It was a very disruptive experience where I was under attack by the Ravens, as many companies are who find that their market has shifted or sales are declining. I wrestled with the problem until someone showed me an opportunity hole in the grid. If I'd have known what was coming I could have redirected my journey much earlier without the stress. I could have bent the elbow just a little and been okay. It is interesting how these things seem parallel."

Rabbit tended his wounds and had a restless niet.

Wednesday – June 10

The next day, Rabbit slept late and was slow to get moving. He finally got to the road and continued. Up ahead he saw that the road leave the grasslands and began to ascend into rocky hills. It was slow moving, for he was still pretty weak. Late in the morning, he was approaching the top of a rugged pass. He paused at the summit to see if he could tell what lay ahead and wondered how much further it could be.

He noticed that the rocky ridges continued for some distance and then fell away. He could not see much further than that and so slowly pressed forward. Occasionally, he would see birds flying overhead and various animals off in the distance or passing by him in the other direction.

By late afternoon he reached a section of terrain that had treacherous cliffs. He had to traverse back and forth along the narrow road as he descended. At one switch-back he saw a sign that read: 'Fountain of spring water.' He could not resist and so followed the path that lead away from the road. Eventually, he came to a rocky outcropping with a bubbling spring pouring out of a crevice, down the face of the rock, and into a waterfall that fell at some distance to a pile of jagged and crushed rocks.

The water was absolutely delicious and he took as much as he could hold. He felt refreshed and renewed for his journey. As he turned to leave he saw a Snake positioned directly in his path back toward the road.

"May I help you," the Snake said quietly.

Something about the Snake sent a chill thrue Rabbit's body. "No I think I'll just return to the road and be on my way.

"Very well," the Snake said and moved to the side of the path so Rabbit could pass.

As Rabbit was moving slowly by the Snake, he heard a noise and turned as the Snake was upon him.

He was suddenly wrapped in massive coils of gripping pressure. He pounded with his feet and forced himself back and forth from side to side trying to free himself, but Snake only increased his pressure.

Frantically, Rabbit squirmed and pawed at the Snake and the ground. The two rolled in a death grip that began to take all the life from Rabbit. He blacked out.

When he came to, he was grasping for air and feeling the waite of the Snake lying across his body. He struggled to get his feet up so he could push the limp Snake away. He lay gasping at the precious air in deep nurturing breaths. When he could finally move he crawled away from the Snake and examined where he was.

The Snake lay motionless and still. As Rabbits eyes moved toward Snakes head he saw that it was split open and the point of a large knife like rock protruding thrue it. He looked up to see the source of a long waterfall splash down not far from him. In his death roll he must have edged the Snake over the cliff and fallen to the rocks below. Landing as they had, he had being cushioned by the coils of the Snake's body, but the Snake had not been as fortunate.

He backed away from the scene and shinnied up and over several rocks. It would be a long climb back up to the path and it took him the rest of the afternoon to get there. When he was back on the road he cautiously continued, keeping an eye out for any suspicious characters that miet be lurking along the way. Rabbit never realized there were such unexpected hazards in the world, outside of Forest Deep.

That niet his sleep was deep and profound. He was exhausted and dreamt of places far away where his friends greeted him. He saw Raccoon and Skunk in his dream and imagined they were whiling away warm summer days by a stream, free from---'suffocation.'

Thursday – June 11

The next morning was filled with restlessness. He wondered how much further it could be. He needed to be back within the week to report to Owl and he wondered exactly what magic he was supposed to demonstrate.

He wanted to hurry, but he was cautious. There apparently were dangers at the least expected times. As he left the rocky hills, he found himself on a broad dry plain. Up until now he had seen very few animals actually coming and going on the road. Now he was encountering occasional travelers in both directions.

By lunch time, he had traveled a good distance and stopped for a rest. All at once he sensed something moving toward him from off the road. As he turned he could see a large Tortoise. The fellow was ponderously slow as could be expected.

"Hello," The Tortoise extended.

"Hello," Rabbit replied.

"Do you mind if I rest beside you for a moment?" Tortoise asked.

"Not a bit. Pull up a rock."

"Where are you headed?" Tortoise asked.

"I'm on my way to see Big-Dog," Rabbit relied.

"Well, you haven't far to go."

"Do you think I'll be there soon?" Rabbit queried.

"You should be there by this evening, without question."

"Perhaps I can rest a few minutes then. I've covered a lot of ground this morning. Where are you headed?" Rabbit inquired.

"I'm going to visit with the manager of my production facility," Tortoise responded. "We build infrastructures and housings. You know things that provide protection from the elements."

"What is your position with the company?" Rabbit wanted to know.

"I'm the CEO riet now, but I'm thinking of grooming one of the younger employees to take my place," Tortoise offered. "It's a challenge to find just the riet person. I think we've stagnated and need to look forward to changes that are coming our way."

"Stagnated?" Rabbit pressed.

"Yes, there haven't been many changes in our industry for a long time. If you produced basic quality products---that is all you really needed to do. Now there are new materials and techniques being introduced. A lot of them are coming from places very distant from here, but they are beginning to have an impact on us."

"I guess they are creating an opportunity-hole in the grid," Rabbit posed.

"What's an opportunity hole?"

"Oh, nothing really, just something I came across recently. So your company hasn't changed much?"

"We have been so stable and profitable for so many years, we haven't had to really worry about change."

"Haven't you had employees offer some new ideas from time to time?" Rabbit wondered.

"You have to understand the nature of the company. Most major changes require a huge investment of resources. We allow employees to spontaneously fine-tune the little things, but when it comes to the big things we have a very formal process. Proposals are strictly screened. First, they have to conform to stringent managerial guidelines. Second, they have to be consistent within the corporate culture and the way we do things. Third, they must demonstrate a low level of risk. When it comes riet down to it, I pretty much know what's best for the company and what proposals we will accept."

"Tell me about the production manager you are going to visit. What type of person is he?" Rabbit inquired.

"He is a lot like me. He is a first rate company man and his ideas are very consistent with the way I think. He very well could be our next president."

"Can I ask a stupid question?" Rabbit admitted.

"Go ahead."

"Have there been any employees that have come up with radical ideas for change in the past?"

"Yea, but they soon learn that you don't upset the apple cart when it's making a good profit."

"I really wonder how you are ever going to change." Rabbit stated.

"What do you mean?" Tortoise recoiled.

"You're company seems a lot like a fellow I met yesterday. Both of you have strangulation on the mind."

"I resent that! We are a great company and will continue to be great. I'm sure it is hard for someone who doesn't really know much about our company to pass judgment on it. Good day," Tortoise said in a huff and continued on his way.

Rabbit sketched a diagram:

CONTROL-CREATIVITY TRADEOFF

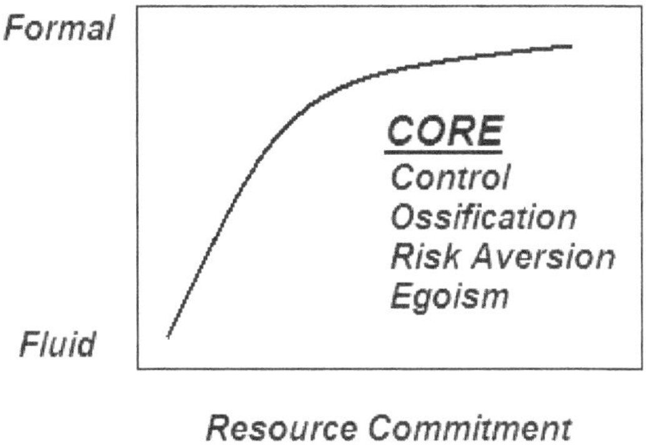

Fluid ideas are fine if no resources are required, but as significant dollar resources are needed the process becomes very formal and four things seem to happen:

1. **Control**: Those who succeed in management are those who comply: look like the old management, think the same way and do the same things. Creative types are mavericks and viewed as disruptive, non-supportive and very seldom promoted.

2. **Ossification**: Bones harden with age. The same is true of the organization: culture becomes more entrenched and past success is hard to deviate from. What worked in the past suffocates new ideas.

3. **Risk Aversion**: New ideas and changes are risky. Dynamic and untested ideas could fail and cause a loss of revenue and deterioration in the bottom line. If the wrong course is selected, disaster could be the result.

4. **Egoism**: Even in the best efforts of group think, aggressive types dominate with "their" ideas: if anyone gets credit and is promoted, it must be them. When the boss is always riet, can any change break thrue.

It seemed like the Tortoise really was slow moving. Then Rabbit stopped. He was criticizing Tortoise and his methods, what about his own. After a little self inspection, Rabbit wondered if his own penchant for quick bursts of energy and change could also be disruptive. A simple truth seemed to be:

Self-centered ossification stifles growth.

The word 'Balance' rolled over and over in his mind. Balance between fluid and formal. Balance between stability and change. Balance between slow and plodding and bursts of energy.

Rabbit continued his journey and eventually came to a rise in the road. Over the rise was a broad clearing filled with various types of cottages and natural structures that lay before him. Everyone was hard at work on every kind of product that could be imagined. There were toys, appliances, furniture, clothing, and vehicles. It was a community of total diversity with every kind of animal working alongside every other.

Rabbit interrupted a passing worker: "Excuse me, but could you tell me how to find Big-Dog."

The little fuzzy worker stopped and pointed to an office at one end of the street: "He's riet over there."

Rabbit couldn't believe that his journey was almost over and hurried toward the office. When he got there, he knocked on the door and was ushered into see Big-Dog. "Hello, I'm Rabbit from Forest Deep." As Rabbit issued his greeting he couldn't help noticing that Big-Dog seemed very old and gray.

"I've been waiting for you: Owl said you would be coming. How has the journey been?" Big-Dog inquired.

"It has been very interesting. I've encountered several different situations along the way that have been both instructive and challenging. But that is of no consequence. I've come to you to learn the 'Magic' of creating value in a business."

"So you have. Before we get to that I want to learn everything about how you came to be selected as the new CEO and every detail about all that you have encountered since."

The rest of the evening Rabbit related everything that had happened. He talked about his Valuation Model and his theory of Organic Finance. He talked about each of the animals he had interfaced with back at Red Maple Mill and along the way. All of his analysis was revealed in very descriptive detail. The interview continued late into the niet.

Finally, Big-Dog said: "It is late and you have filled me with wonderful thawts. Do you mind if we rest for the niet and continue our discussion tomorrow?"

"No, that would be fine," Rabbit responded. That niet his mind was filled with dreams and imaginings about all the amazing things Big-Dog would tell him the next day.

Friday – June 12

After breakfast Big-Dog and Rabbit went walking thrue the maze of operations that were in full swing. "I really like the work you've done on your valuation model and think that an organic approach to value is riet on the mark. You have observed that an organic company is a growing company and to grow a company has to change. Unfortunately, change is constantly being evaluated within the constraints of earnings and risk. If everyone could do it, they would. It is not easy and so searching for the riet combination within each business is a challenge. What have you learned that you will take back with you to Forest Deep?" Big-Dog asked.

"I'm more than ever convinced there needs to be balance in the organization. Employees at every level need to be able to express fluid ideas and have the organization evaluate them seriously. I think that will create an environment of hie energy workers. Companies should not exert such heavy control that they suffocate potential. A company also needs to be constantly searching for opportunity holes and early redirection so the changes are sliet and not traumatic," Rabbit said with conviction. That requires an early information system.

"Do you think a single individual at the top of an organization can cause this to happen?" Big-Dog inquired.

"I don't know. What is the 'Magic' then?" Rabbit asked.

"I hope this journey has tawt you one thing: that there is no easy prescription or magic dust that you can sprinkle on any situation and make it perfect. Miracles happen when leaders have faith and work hard. In the absence of that, they begin to look for magic or mystical unexplainable prestidigitations. I hope you have learned that "miracles" happen when you are calm and assertive, as you listen and learn. Never be afraid to admit that you don't know and be constantly searching for answers."

Rabbit sat in rapt fascination. Big-Dog was an imposing figure and commanded respect and attention. Rabbit wondered if he could ever become such a leader. Finally, Rabbit pressed for a more specific appraisal of Big-Dog's opinion regarding his valuation theory: "What do you think of the valuation model I'm proposing?"

"It sounds wonderful. As a mater-of-fact, it reflects my personal philosophy for success."

Rabbit couldn't believe his ears. "What is your philosophy?"

<u>The Big Dogma</u> "Market Power insures Earnings; Adaptive Leadership fosters Growth; and Advance Information reduces Risk."

"It involves three concepts: First, Earnings will always be a struggle unless you have Market Power. If you do, then you can control your environment enuf to generate the earnings you need."

"Second, you must be an Adaptive Leader who fosters innovation, change, and growth. Living things grow because they adapt to their environment."

"Third, it is critical that you obtain Advance Information before your competitors. That is the sure way to reduce risk. If you know what is coming early enuf then life becomes so much more manageable."

"All of the experiences you have had coming here have reinforced these concepts in one way or another," Big-Dog observed.

"What do you mean?" Rabbit asked.

"The difficulties you had with the Crows and the Snake could have been avoided if you had known what to look for. This comes from experience, study, and agents. Other people will provide you with information if you know how to cultivate them," Big-Dog counseled.

Rabbit was overwhelmed. He spent the rest of the day with Big-Dog as they discussed many things. At one point Big-Dog explained a more tactical approach: "The emphasis must be placed on Customer, Employee, and Resources, in that order.

Satisfy the customer where the opportunity holes exist. Don't suffocate the employee: let them express fluid ideas and then review them in a formal process. Resources must then be marshaled to energize Employees to serve the Customer.

At one point Rabbit asked: "Your company appears to be extremely successful, people are productive and everything seems to work so well. I can understand the focus on the Customer and listening to the Employees, but there has to be something more."

Big-Dog continued: "You can make things complicated or simple and I think simple is best. In business, everything comes down to the simple relationship between benefit and cost. Does the benefit justify the cost? My job has always been to communicate to the employees, in terms they understand, about the benefits and costs. If I do that they respond. So I'm always trying to figure out ways to communicate the message. In the employee's mind, it is a decision of how much effort do they expend. Change takes an inordinate amount of effort. In this business, I don't manage, I lead by communicating.

"But how?" Rabbit wanted to know.

"I would propose that communicating is everything that is good about marketing and nothing that is bad. It is positive and encouraging. It is not the spinning of slogans, or making false claims to gain a momentary edge or make the sale. Honest communication is speaking the truth."

Big-Dog continued: “I reward new ideas, I reward team participation, and I share the results of success. Employees can be a drag on the company or they can be its greatest asset: it totally depends on how the company treats them. A lot of that is the attitude of the company’s leader. I celebrate the work of all the employees, but only as it helps with the ultimate service to the customer. This is not new and it’s not complicated, but a lot of businesses just don’t seem to understand. The secret to your success as the “Leader” will be to continually mold the vision that steers the company toward the opportunity holes you can reasonably serve with the company’s expertise and resources. Then be active in communicating the message to everyone.”

“As you innovate you must always strive for Early Information that leads to Innovation and Growth that will in turn result in Market Power. Your biggest asset is your ability to listen. I believe you will do very well.”

“Do you think you can utilize your valuation model and tell me what you think my company is worth?” Big Dog asked.

As Rabbit extracted the three elements needed for the model he found the normalized earnings estimate and projected growth to be very strong. On the other hand the risk adjusted interest rate the company was paying on its debt was very low. “This must be the perfect company,” Rabbit said as he gave Big Dog the valuation. “What do you think of the number?”

"That is incredible. You have focused on the essence of the numbers and they look good, but remember that the numbers are only a reflection of all that a company is," Big Dog instructed.

That niet Rabbit was so full of ideas that he could hardly sleep. It had been a wonderful day and the end of a very educational week.

Saturday – June 13

The next day as Rabbit was about to set off, he expressed his concern about getting home in two days when it had taken him so long coming. Big-Dog said: "Over that hill is a river. If you catch a boat there, it will take you to a place that is within half a day's walk from Forest Deep."

Rabbit bid farewell to Big-Dog and did as he was instructed. He found the river and was able to catch a small passenger boat operated by two Muskrats. He found a comfortable spot on deck and relaxed as the countryside passed by.

At one point along the journey the boat stopped and several passengers climbed aboard. They sat quietly about the deck taking in some liet refreshment. Rabbit looked around and counted five other passengers. One was a rather impressive looking Wolverine who was very intimidating.

Rabbit had come to realize that he had learned a great deal simply by talking to people, so after walking about the deck a bit he sat down by

Wolverine "How far are you going?" Rabbit confidently asked, leveraging his experience that a good conversation always began with a question that exhibited some real interest.

"All the way to Aspen Grove; there is a company there I'm going to look at."

"Look at?" Rabbit puzzled.

"I maintain a portfolio of investments and am continually looking for good companies."

Rabbit could hardly believe his good luck. He had been talking with a lot of company executives, but this was someone who was an external investor. "I've just been elected to the post of Chairman of the Board and Leader of Red Maple Mill at Forest Deep. It would be a real treat to find out what investors look at to determine a great company."

"We are not all the same. Some look at numbers or trends. I look at other things."

Rabbit was ecstatic, someone who was interested in how the company was actually run and not just the financial results. "I'm a little hesitant to ask and don't want you to reveal any secrets, but what other things do you look at?"

"I've shared this with many people, but they don't seem to understand. You look like a fellow who listens. I'll give you my ten rules of a great company:

1. Do products generate competitive advantage?
2. Are new products being developed?
3. Is research and development effective?

4. Is the sales organization above average?
5. Is a strong profit margin maintained?
6. Are company people treated well?
7. Are cost analysis/accounting controls in place?
8. Is the company superior to its competition?
9. Can growth come without external financing?
10. Is management of unquestioned integrity?

"I've found this is an excellent way to evaluate a company."

"Are they ranked in the order of their importance?" Rabbit asked.

"No---not really; it's just a check-list that I use."

"I guess the optimal question would be: Has this approach resulted in satisfactory performance," Rabbit queried.

"It all depends on what your goals are. I'm a long-term value investor and so it has been excellent," Wolverine said proudly.

"That's wonderful. Can I show you a methodology I've worked out for determining value? It is a formula, but I like to show a diagram." Rabbit produced his value triangle chart. "I propose that value is a function of normalized earnings, a combination of long-term growth and short-term growth, and the risk of the company as measured by its risk-adjusted interest rate. What do you think?"

"You've nailed all the critical issues. It says 'organic' in the middle, what does that represent?"

"I think it represents exactly what you are talking about. A company must have sufficient controls in place to regulate the company, but is hiely growth oriented. It treats its people well and management has integrity. I think your check-list of ten things compliments my approach very well," Rabbit said excitedly.

"You may have something there. You say it is a formula?" Wolverine pressed.

Rabbit rehearsed his formula and how it could be used to calculate value. Wolverine seemed relatively interested and the discussion continued for some time. Eventually, Rabbit sensed that Wolverine was tiring and so he excused himself, walk about the boat and settled back in the chair he originally occupied.

As he reflected on everything that had happened during the last several days he tried to catalogue all that he had learned. He needed to prepare for the challenges ahead that faced Red Maple Mill. How could he prepare for uncertain events? How could he gain advance information to reduce risk? How could he be a leader who adapts? How could he gain market power? He was jolted back to reality as the boat rolled slietly. Was he prepared for this trip?

He stood up and wandered back to where one of the Muskrats was tending some ropes. "Do you mind if I ask you a question?" Rabbit asked.

"What do you need?"

"I was curious about our journey. Do we pass any points of interest along the way?" Rabbit queried.

"It's relatively uneventful."

vas below his chair. After clicking his straps in he looked around to see the other passengers ng on for dear life.

e was about to go to their assistance when a ive rock appeared out of nowhere. The boat was ied against the rock and its crumbled side gave to a rush of foaming water. Rabbit was suddenly bbing cork in a violent thrashing of waves and s.

e was thrust against a frantic body struggling to afloat. Rabbit grabbed an arm and held on for life. Ten minutes of terror passed and the storm e at the same time the rapids melted away into water.

abbit kicked his way to the side of the river and nuddy bank. The arm he had been clutching was ected to a huge mass that Rabbit struggled to ahead of him to the shore. It was Wolverine.

lay – June 14

he two water logged survivors were lonely ps on the bank of the river. Wolverine said ing and Rabbit could not tell if he was thankful Rabbit's help or so overcome with exhaustion he could not muster any interaction.

Rabbit's thawts were drawn to the accident and fortunate he was to have put on the life erver. He was beginning to anticipate future its and it saved his life. Big Dog had said that vance Information Reduces Risk.' How could a

"So I really don't need to
find a life-preserver or anyth
continued.

"All the life-preservers ar
We used to go thrue the rapic
them, as we go by way of a c
that is separated from the ma
after the rapids. So there is nc
We have been over this route
Muskrat said.

"When do we get to the cl

"It will be late---a little be

"I'm headed to Forest Dec
should get off?" Rabbit press

"You need to get off at the
get there about mid-morning.

"Thanks for the informati
returned to his seat.

It was around eleven o'clo
started blowing. Soon it was f
storm. The canopy over the de
protection from the pounding
swept across the boat horizont
anchored himself to a post, he
the two Muskrats frantically tı
vessel. They were doing all th
check and had little time to ca

The storm increased in inte
couple of hours. As the boat rc
and forth, Rabbit struggled to

that was below his chair. After clicking his straps in place he looked around to see the other passengers holding on for dear life.

He was about to go to their assistance when a massive rock appeared out of nowhere. The boat was crushed against the rock and its crumbled side gave way to a rush of foaming water. Rabbit was suddenly a bobbing cork in a violent thrashing of waves and rocks.

He was thrust against a frantic body struggling to stay afloat. Rabbit grabbed an arm and held on for dear life. Ten minutes of terror passed and the storm broke at the same time the rapids melted away into calm water.

Rabbit kicked his way to the side of the river and to a muddy bank. The arm he had been clutching was connected to a huge mass that Rabbit struggled to push ahead of him to the shore. It was Wolverine.

Sunday – June 14

The two water logged survivors were lonely lumps on the bank of the river. Wolverine said nothing and Rabbit could not tell if he was thankful for Rabbit's help or so overcome with exhaustion that he could not muster any interaction.

Rabbit's thawts were drawn to the accident and how fortunate he was to have put on the life preserver. He was beginning to anticipate future events and it saved his life. Big Dog had said that 'Advance Information Reduces Risk.' How could a

"So I really don't need to know where I would find a life-preserver or anything like that?" Rabbit continued.

"All the life-preservers are underneath your seats. We used to go thrue the rapids, but now we bypass them, as we go by way of a channel of calm water that is separated from the main river and then returns after the rapids. So there is nothing to worry about. We have been over this route hundreds of times," the Muskrat said.

"When do we get to the channel?"

"It will be late---a little before midniet."

"I'm headed to Forest Deep. When do you think I should get off?" Rabbit pressed anxiously.

"You need to get off at the Log-on-End stop. We get there about mid-morning."

"Thanks for the information." With that Rabbit returned to his seat.

It was around eleven o'clock when the wind started blowing. Soon it was followed by a violent storm. The canopy over the deck was some protection from the pounding rains, but the water swept across the boat horizontally. As Rabbit anchored himself to a post, he looked around to see the two Muskrats frantically trying to control the vessel. They were doing all they could to keep it in check and had little time to care for the passengers.

The storm increased in intensity for the next couple of hours. As the boat rocked violently back and forth, Rabbit struggled to find the life-preserver business get advance information? Then he thawt about exchange as a basic tenant of an organic business: not just exchange of money and products, but of ideas and information. Who were those who could increase this conduit of advance information?

Rabbit began to think about all the sources of potential information and to make a list from his personal reflections and experience. The result was a diagram that he called "SPACE MAP." The most obvious sources were the vertical relationships from Suppliers to Purchasers along the chain of the product from source to end user. Next, were the horizontal relationships in the marketplace where Associations (trade) and Competitors were found. Beyond these sources came information from what was called the Environment or IMAGE: investor activity, media buzz, analyst's research, governmental actions, and economic conditions.

SPACE & IMAGE

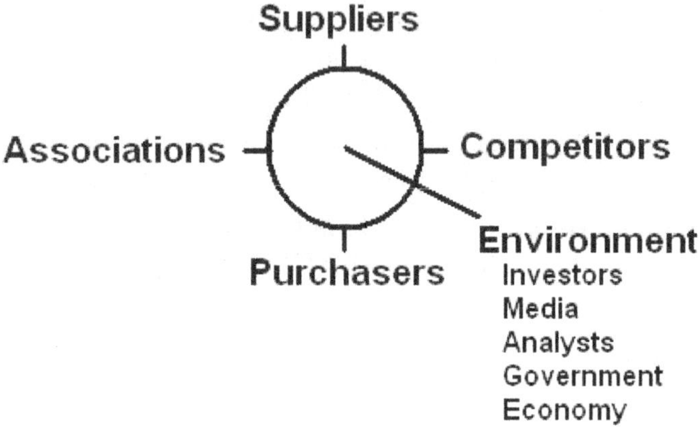

He realized there was a definite art in how one would extract information and keep it confidential. It was all beginning to come together. He would be much more active in external exchange, sifting of data, and gathering critical "advance information" on possible opportunity holes and potential risks. This could help the company recognize market situations.

Then Rabbit wondered about market situations and how to gain what Big Dog talked about as 'Market Strength.' The market was so complex and dynamic. Was the whole secret just putting customers first and giving them valued service. Rabbit had to concentrate on maters at hand…how was he going to get home?

By late morning, Swan, in a small boat coming down the river, spotted two figures standing on the bank. They looked like two refugees from a zoo. One was Wolverine and the other Rabbit. The two were invited into the boat.

"Have you seen anyone else along the way?" Rabbit inquired.

"Not a soul. You're the only two individuals I've seen all morning," Swan said.

It was a quiet trip to the Log-on-End stop. Rabbit slept most of the way. At the Log-on-End, he left Wolverine and Swan, expressing gratitude for all their kindness. It was late evening and he still had half a day's trek to get back to the Gnarly Oak and his appointed meeting with Owl.

As Rabbit trudged toward home he encountered a large Bullfrog hopping along the same path. "Where are you headed?" Rabbit asked.

"I'm headed to The Meadow of Seven Streams."

"Don't you have to go thrue Forest Deep to get there?" Rabbit asked.

"I do."

"Do you mind if I travel that far with you?"

"Not at all, but you'll have to keep up. I drive a hard pace," Bullfrog emphasized as he leaped forward.

Rabbit was with him and they began to match hop for hop. "Why are you in such a hurry to get to the Meadow?"

"I'm supposed to give a lecture to a group on 'The various kinds of markets they will encounter.' But I inadvertently put it on my calendar for next week and when I realized the error it was late in the afternoon and so I'm going to have to travel all niet long," Bullfrog explained as he made another giant leap across a little brook.

"What do you mean by 'Kinds of Markets'? Are you an expert on markets?" Rabbit fired off two questions in quick succession as he cleared the same brook.

Answering the questions in reverse order, Bullfrog responded: "I'm what you would call a consultant in the marketing field and I have a rather unusual approach to evaluating markets. I've divided markets into six types and how to deal with them."

Rabbit and Bullfrog conversed all along the trail and after long explanation the six markets were disclosed to Rabbit. When Bullfrog bid farewell at the Forest Deep to continue his journey, Rabbit made a quick summary of all he had learned:

1. **Accessible Markets**: Enter before the competition with a superior brand and image, and carefully guard your relationships with suppliers. Then you will be able to compete with advantage.
2. **Entangling Markets**: These may be abandoned, but may be hard to re-enter and so are called entangling. If the competition is unprepared, they may be easily displaced.
3. **Temporized Markets**: When neither competitor can gain the edge by making the first move, hold back, waiting for the

competition to revealing their position to be challenged with advantage.

4. **Niche Markets**: if first in place, then protect aggressively. If a competitor is first with a dominate market share, it may be unprofitable to enter. Only enter if the competitor is vulnerable.
5. **Exclusive**: If in a priority position with dominant brand: promote the image aggressively. If the competition has preference, the only option is to entice them away from their position.
6. **Foreign**: It may be difficult to challenge a competitor that is equally resourced. This situation must be carefully analyzed and evaluated, before any action is taken.

Rabbit began to wonder just what kind of market the Forest Deep had been involved in and what new markets it miet face.

Monday – June 15

Rabbit arrived at his home just before day-break. He quickly freshened up, changed his clothes, and grabbed a bit of food. He got to Gnarly Oak a few minutes early and was prepared when Owl made his descent from the sky.

"I see you've made it," Owl was pleased.

"I've had an unbelievable education in the last seven days," Rabbit responded.

“Did you find Big-Dog?

“Yes, and he was very helpful.”

“I’m not going to ask you to tell me all that happened, but I’m sure it was just what you needed. Are you ready to assume a leadership role?” Owl wanted to know.

“I’d like to ask a favor”

“What is that?” Owl said curiously.

“I know that you are pretty well connected in the business community. Is there an industry expert that miet come and brief the board of trends they are seeing?”

Owl thawt for a moment: “Seagull is probably the best I can think of. I’ll see if I can’t get him to come?”

“The sooner he gets here the better. I’d like to call a meeting of the board for tomorrow,” Rabbit responded.

“I’ll see what I can do.”

“Thank you,” Rabbit expressed.

The meeting was soon over and Owl jumped into the air and was off.

New Leadership

(The fable concludes)

Rabbit sent out word that there was to be an emergency board meeting the next day. Then he went to Red Maple Mill to meet with Beaver: the Chief Operating Officer and Otter: the Chief Financial Officer. He spent the rest of the day going over Red Maple Mill's operating and financial reports and projections. It was very late that evening when he finished with Beaver and Otter. He invited both of them to the board meeting the next day.

Tuesday – June 16

The next morning Rabbit greeted each of the board members as they arrived at the Gnarly Oak. He let them mingle for a few moments and then began by ascending to the large lower limb and calling them to attention

"I want to thank you for coming. It has only been a little over a week since I was placed in this position, but I feel that I've been schooled already. I would like to begin by reviewing what our charge is."

"The Board of Directors is primarily responsible to external stakeholders for oversiet. You set strategic direction; approve financial goals and capital structure; select and evaluate senior management; are accountable for performance;

insure ethical conduct, compliance with laws, adequate internal controls, and the independence of external auditors."

"At Red Maple Mill the positions of chairman-of-the-board and CEO have been invested in the same person. Management of the company has been delegated to the Chief Executive Officer. Board members have had a broad range of backgrounds and experience. From time to time, the company has called upon board members as advocates to represent the company in the community. The board has also provided an excellent network with other companies and groups that could impact the company.

I think in all regards we have adequately fulfilled our responsibilities. Rabbit then placed an hour glass on the limb.

> <u>The Hour-Glass Model</u>
> "All information is funneled thrue the CEO."

"We have acted much like this hour-glass and it was entirely appropriate. The Board would be represented by the bulb at the top. As we set policy we would direct the CEO to carry that forward. He, represented by the narrow neck in the middle, would then transport our message to the operational part of Red Maple Mill, represented by the bulb at the bottom," Rabbit said.

Rabbit then turned the hour-glass over and the grains of sand began to fall from top to bottom. "Now, as Red Maple Mill operated, its information would be taken by the CEO back to the board. Everything passed thrue the CEO. This is not a problem it is simply a representation of how it has been. In most cases, I would like to continue to operate under the Hour-Glass Model."

"Let me turn to the recent performance of Red Maple Mill. Beaver, Otter, and I spent a long time yesterday going over current trends. For a long time we have seen a gradual increase in earnings of around 6% per year. Our sales volume has been flat, but we have seen a steady rise in revenue as the result of price increases. We have bumped up prices to compensate for inflation pressure on expenses. Revenue went up 6% per year and earnings followed. We have been extremely predictable and a very safe company."

"About a year ago thing began to change. Inflation was still in the 6% range, but the volume of products that we have been selling has dropped. This decline in sales volume has offset our price increases and so revenue has been flat this past year. Beaver tells me the marketing department has projected there will be an accelerating decline in the demand for our shingles. The market is starting to use other types of materials: plastic, fiberglass, metal, and composites. It appears that the world has changed and we have been slow to adjust," Rabbit reported calmly but firmly.

The members of the board became restless. They had never experienced this kind of talk from their

CEO before. "Are you sure the numbers are riet?" Fox wanted to know.

"I would be delieted if you would lend some of your expertise to verify them," Rabbit responded.

"This can't be. I've been on this board for years and have never heard such talk. You haven't changed the way we account for various things have you?" Gander demanded.

"Perhaps our Chief Financial Officer could answer that question," Rabbit said turning the attention to Otter.

"There have been no changes in our accounting policies or in the way we put the reports together," Otter resolutely stated.

"Our bankers aren't going to like this," Porcupine noted.

"Did you say an accelerating decline? What does that mean?" Skunk pressed.

"I think within three to five years we will be out of the shingle business altogether," Rabbit noted.

There was an audible gasp from the members of the board. Then they broke into a buzz of side-bars and individual conversations. Rabbit overheard Raccoon say to Beaver: "How come Owl never told us this? Maybe Rabbit is in a little over his head."

Rabbit had always considered Raccoon to be one of his best friends, but this little remark hurt. He held his composure and wondered to himself if those we are closest too have the hardest time accepting us in a new position.

"May I have your attention," Rabbit raised his voice to gain control of the meeting, maintaining a calm and firm demeanor. "I know this is awfully sudden, riet on the heals of a leadership change, but I can assure you our position in the market place is a fact the operating personnel are very aware of. I can't explain why we haven't heard this before, but I wanted you to know as soon as possible."

"What are we going to do about it?" Gander demanded.

"Let me just say that the company is not going out of business in the near future. We are going to find ways to not only keep going, but grow," Rabbit responded.

"Growth has been very difficult for us in the past. We have a limited amount of resource. The trees we harvest are on a very systematic schedule. We replant everything we cut to ensure a hundred year model of equilibrium and replacement," Fox offered. "We have looked at the productive capacity of our forest and there is no additional volume without compromising something."

Rabbit knew it was critical for him to continue to look as thoe he was comfortably in charge and assured of himself. "We have always operated under the goal of 'Predictable Increasing Earnings'. That will be our goal in the future."

"I never knew that was our goal," Raccoon scoffed.

"It was never put into those exact terms, but if you think about it, that is what we always expected," Ferret cut in.

Rabbit placed a diagram on the Gnarly Oak as he began to speak.

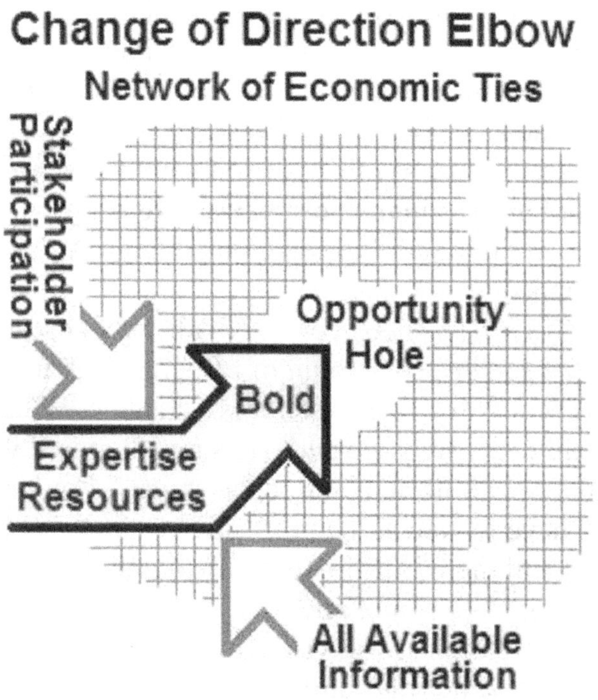

"This past week, at Owl's invitation, I traveled to see one of his mentors: Big-Dog. I had an interesting trip and encountered some very challenging experiences. I met a Bloodhound struggling with some of the same problems we are confronting. He showed me a model that I think is very applicable in our situation."

"This is called 'Change of Direction Elbow'. We function in a market within the Network of Economic Ties. It is filled with a network of interconnecting expectations, wants, and needs that are satisfied by many businesses. The inter-relationships are continually changing. We have been very comfortable for a long time, but suddenly our path along the grid is beginning to narrow and may close altogether. We need to adapt and change directions slietly."

"The quicker we identify where there is an opportunity hole, the less dramatic our change will be. We carry with us our Expertise and Resources: they are wonderful assets that need to be leveraged for our success. The way we change is thrue stakeholder participation and tapping into all available information. I miet suggest that we also must keep in mind the wonderful resources that our employees, suppliers, and the environment provide. We will focus on energizing our effort and expand our exchange and interchange with all points of contact. We can do this," Rabbit assured.

The board members studied the chart for some time. "What does the word 'Bold' signify?" Skunk asked.

"When we find the path to follow we will pursue it aggressively and with boldness," Rabbit came back. "Just remember it must be within the constraints of 'Predictable Increasing Earnings'.

"What is an 'Opportunity Hole'?" Ferret said pointing to the middle of the chart.

"The market is constantly changing as the economy, technology, and expectations change. As it shifts holes appear where customers are seeking new and better products and services. Old connections are strained and new opportunities emerge. Innovative companies can move in to meet those needs. If we are vigilant, we can completely satisfy, if not exceed, those customer's demands. It is the place where we can find Predictable Increasing Earnings," Rabbit explained.

There was still an air of apprehension surrounding the board members when all at once Ferret offered: "I'm with you. What do you want us to do?"

"We need new ideas and collaboration. I don't have a corner on the best ideas, they could come from anywhere. We need to put into place a process for change. I'd like to propose, what I call the 'Wicker-Basket Model'." Rabbit placed a basket, full of all kinds of delicious food, on the Gnarly Oak.

"A Wicker-Basket is constructed by first placing a solid base with vertical strands extending upward from points equally spaced around the base. The base represents our unified mission. I would compare these strands to each of you board members. Then wicker is woven in and out of the vertical strands in a network type weave to form the basket. I would compare these horizontal strands to information and ideas that may come from every possible source."

"When the basket is completed it is tied together, at the top, with a braid of interconnecting wicker that makes it a strong structure. The basket can hold a lot of delicious things which I hope will be all the wonderful ideas for redirecting our company toward opportunity holes," Rabbit explained.

Wicker-Basket Model "Stakeholders work with all sources of information to harvest new and creative ideas."

"The Hour-Glass Model separates functional areas of the board from operations. The Wicker-Basket Model integrates all areas into teams of dynamic exploration. It has been my experience that some of the very best ideas come inside as well as outside the organization. I have developed what I call the SPACE MAP:

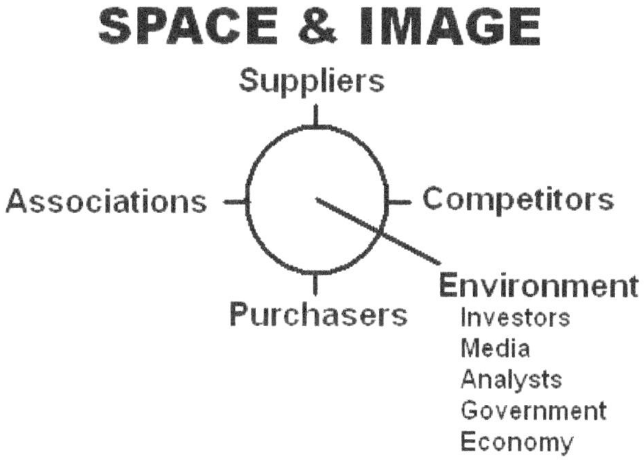

This shows all the possible external contacts and sources of information. In addition we will listen to those within the organization, the employees. I want to provide a fluid opportunity for all ideas to be heard and evaluated."

"How would it work?" Raccoon asked cynically.

"I'd like to propose that each board member become an integral part of the information network. Each of you will take on three functional roles. First, you will take one of the letters from the SPACE acronym. For example raccoon may be assigned suppliers as his primary responsibility and he will gather every possible bit of information from our various providers of materials and supplies. Skunk miet take customers and do extensive surveying to determine the needs and demands of those who consume goods. Gander miet take our trade associations and Porcupine take our competitors.

Second, each will take one of the letters from the IMAGE acronym: Investors, Media, Analysts, Government, and Economic Indicators. Some will have both a SPACE and IMAGE assignment and others miet only have one.

Third, each of you will head up an employee committee that incorporates employees from various departments and brainstorm on new ideas for the company. These employee committees will also explore external sources of information looking for areas that are opening up and underserved. I think the ideas should focus on new opportunities in the market and how our expertise and resources can be redeployed in more innovative ways. I've spoken to Beaver and Otter and they agree this could be very interesting. I would give each of you a list of names and it would be up to you to coordinate these teams. I think we could end up with a real basket full of great suggestions."

There was some grumbling as Board Members fussed over the idea of extra work. Just as Rabbit was about to deal with their concerns, Gander interjected and gestured toward the sky: "What's that?"

Everyone looked up to spot a bird descending toward them. As it got closer they could all determine that it was a Seagull. Landing just outside of the circle of the board, Seagull waited to be recognized.

"Are you the industry analyst that Owl was going to send?" Rabbit asked.

"I certainly am and I had to drop everything to get here. Owl was pretty insistent that I come," Seagull said.

"That is wonderful." Turning to the board, Rabbit continued: "I asked Owl to send us an industry expert to give us an outside perspective on what is happening. I thawt a little more information couldn't hurt. Let me invite Seagull up and perhaps we can give him the time he needs riet now."

Seagull ascended to the Gnarly Oak and then said: "I'm not sure exactly what it is you would like to know, but I'll begin by saying that my job is to continually analyze the wood products industry. Within that industry are a broad range of products and so I'm not sure just how applicable, what I have to say, will be to your mill."

Fox raised his hand to be recognized. "Excuse me, but we have just learned from our CEO that sales of our wood shingles are beginning to decline and the demand for them could end in the next three to five years. What do you say about that?"

Seagull looked at Rabbit and then back at the members of the board. "I hate to say this, but I think that's exactly what will happen. We are seeing so many more options for our customers that many of them are opting for products made of alternative materials. Wood shingles have been pretty resistant to competition for a long time, but that has changed. With better communications and transportation systems, we are seeing products come from distant regions that we never saw before."

"As a matter of fact, the whole wood products industry is in the same boat. Everything is in transition and those companies that adapt and change are going to survive, those that don't---won't."

"Is it just a question of survival?" Skunk asked.

"In many cases, but I've seen some companies be very aggressive about innovating and are doing well. I've also seen about twenty percent of our companies go under and that number is expected to eventually be as hie as fifty percent."

Members of the board gasped in unison. Seagull continued: "I don't mean to alarm you, but the reality is that we are in a world where you are going to have to change or be eliminated."

"What are the successful companies doing?" Rabbit asked.

"Some are getting out of wood altogether, but most are finding ways to incorporate their wood resources in new and innovative ways. Do you know what I mean when I say composites, laminates, and veneers? Do you know how strong glues and plastics are becoming? Have you looked at alternative applications for some of your waste products? The successful companies are focusing on customer first, but riet behind that are employee, supplier, and the environment. I can't tell you how important communication and transportation are becoming."

"If there was ever a wake-up call, I think we just got it," Porcupine said. "Three to five years is not very long. I feel a great sense of urgency."

"I'm glad we are getting the message, but I feel we can not only survive, but we have the ability to become one of the truly great success stories," Rabbit encouraged. Then turning to Seagull he asked: "Would you be able to spend a little time with us or do you have to rush off?"

"I have a few moments," Seagull responded.

"I'd like to conclude today's board meeting now and give each of you some time to ask Seagull any other questions you miet have. We need to think positively about this opportunity. I hope you will all move forward with your teams. I don't want you to think about the many constraints we face. In this first phase we are open to all and any ideas. In a later phase we will test each idea against our ultimate goal of 'Predictable Increasing Earnings'," Rabbit instructed.

The meeting broke up and Seagull spent time mingling with various Board Members and answering questions. As the last Board Member left, Rabbit thanked Seagull for coming and invited him to stay for lunch. At lunch, Seagull wanted to know where the goal of 'Predictable Increasing Earnings' had come from.

"We have always focused on those things; I simply consolidated them into one goal. To tell you the truth, it is a perversion of a concept that I have developed about how the value of a company is determined. I call it my 'Value Triangle'. In the triangle there are three points that correspond with the goal. 'Earnings' is the same for both the triangle and the goal, but 'Increasing' relates to growth and 'Predictable' is a function of risk."

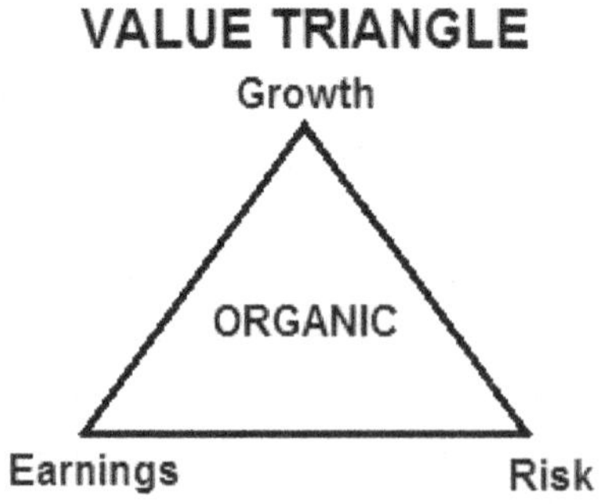

"That's very curious," Seagull noted.

"Actually, I have developed a formula for calculating exactly what the value of a company should be. The formula is $V = E/[.01g^{-(5r+.5)}]$: where E is normalized earnings; g is the average long-term growth rate; and r is the risk adjusted interest rate. It is a lot simpler than most valuation models, but I think it has real merit."

"Have you tested it against real data?" Seagull asked with great interest.

"I have. The correlation wasn't perfect, but it was closer than many other models. I feel very comfortable with it. The biggest challenge in applying any model is trying to determine each variable. I suppose the real challenge is determining the organic nature of the company that supports the models assumptions." Rabbit explained.

"The reason why there may be a difference between the value you calculate and the price of the stock may be simply a hot/not factor," Seagull pointed out.

"The hot/not factor. What is that?"

"Markets are funny things. Price is not only a function of value, but it is also affected by the ebb and flow of people's passions and perceptions. Companies will get 'Hot' and their price will be bid up beyond a justifiable figure. Conversely, Companies that are out of favor for one reason or another will see their stock price fall below what it should be. They just simply are 'Not' popular at the moment. Does the formula work for your company?" Seagull wanted to know.

“It did until I realized that we were in trouble. Based on historical trends we had a pretty consistent growth rate. Next years earnings appeared to be easily determined and we have been so predictable that our risk adjusted interest rate was easily identified.”

“Then what happened?” Seagull pressed.

“Then I looked at the numbers more closely and at the market generally. I received some critical information from our sales and operations people and realized the sun was setting on our products. With a company that has a five year window of declining sales and earnings, there is no long-term trend to insert into the formula.”

“Your chart says ‘Organic’ in the middle, what is that?”

“I think it is critical for a company to have solid organic growth of products and services. A lot of companies grow by acquisition or what turns out to be ‘Smoke and Mirrors’ as they monkey the numbers. I think true value is organic growth of the company’s efforts to meet customer’s needs,” Rabbit proudly said.

“I like what you are doing. I like your model and think I’ll try it out. I just hope you can turn this company in the riet direction and keep it going. If you had more lead time, the change would be easier, but you have been cawt in a crunch to move quickly. I hope it works out.”

After Seagull left, Rabbit had time to reflect on the Board Meeting. He felt good about his approach. He was gathering all the information he could and had solicited input from Board. He had to accept the outcome. He reminded himself to remain Calm and Firm.

Wednesday – June 17

Rabbit was up early and went to Red Maple Mill. He spent time with Beaver and Otter. He wandered around and visited with a lot of the employees. Before he could leave for lunch Beaver cawt up with him and directed him to a room at the back of Red Maple Mill. Bear was waiting for him.

"Isn't this a little unprecedented for the President of the Bank to make a visit to Red Maple Mill?" Rabbit wanted to know.

"When Owl informed me there was a change of leadership, I thawt it best if I come over myself to see how things are going. Transition at the head of any organization can be a very traumatic thing. I wanted to get to know the new leader on a more personal basis. How ARE things going?" Bear asked.

Rabbit firmly believed in complete honesty, but wondered what the implications would be if he were to tell Bear about the results of the Board Meeting. He wondered if this was purely coincidence or if someone from the Board had already met with Bear and this was a test to see if the CEO would corroborate the story. He wondered how much to hold back and how much to reveal. "It has been a very exciting couple of weeks," Rabbit offered.

"I've been telling Owl for some time now that change was inevitable and that he needed to start looking to the future. He is an old-school type manager and has run a pretty tiet ship. I guess he took my advice and decided to move-on rather than see his little baby thrue a repositioning. He tells me you are perfect for the job," Bear stated.

Rabbit knew the bank had always been a partner with Red Maple Mill. They had extended credit whenever it was needed and currently there was a sizable loan to the bank on Red Maple Mill's books. "I appreciate Owl's confidence. I think you are absolutely correct in your assessment of things. A lot of change is needed and we have already launched an aggressive program to take advantage of our expertise and resources in moving forward." Rabbit knew it was important to hit the Board over the head with some alarming statistics to get them moving. Treating the bank the same way miet result in alarm signals that could be negative.

"How are the financial reports looking for the most recent period?" Bear asked.

With that comment, Rabbit indeed wondered if one of the Board members had already been to Bear.

"They appear to be soft."

"Soft!" Bear responded quickly.

"Revenue was flat this past year when compared to the prior year."

"What do you think that means for the future?" Bear pressed.

Rabbit couldn't believe what he was hearing. It was as if Bear already knew the answers and was simply teasing the new CEO to admit it. Rabbit did not want to dangle the five year window in front of the bank president: "I think we have a lot of work to do. We have rolled up our sleeves and jumped riet in."

"How long to you think the market for Wood Shingles will last?"

At last Bear came riet to the point. Rabbit responded: "To be perfectly frank, I project that sales of Wood Shingle, like the ones we currently manufacture, will slowly decline over the next three to five years."

Bear's eyes seemed to pierce Rabbit like a Raven's claw: "That is a problem."

Growth was going to require a major investment of funds to launch the company in a new direction. It was critical that Bear and the bank were on board with the new vision and direction. "We have been consulting with an industry expert and I feel confident we can turn this thing around. We have always appreciated the way your bank has supported us and will need strong backing in the short-term to get thrue this."

"Change can be very risky and the bank is not a risk seeking organization. I was thinking that we miet want to secure the existing loan with some type of note against your forest. In case your plan doesn't materialize at least the bank would be able to get its money back by selling off some of your timber reserves.

Rabbit felt this was the worst answer he could get. He wanted the bank to see the future and all the potential Red Maple Mill had, but instead they were talking about security. "I'm sure that would be no problem at all."

"Good, I'll have my staff draw up the documents and bring them over later in the week," Bear said as he worked his way toward the door.

The visit from Bear was too coincidental on the heels of the Board meeting. One of the Board members must have instigated it, but who would do it?

Rabbit began to understand that changing the direction a company is headed is no easy task. Trying to bring all the various stakeholders together with a single vision of change was becoming very difficult. He was not asking them to boldly go in one direction or another. He was simply trying to begin a process for change.

Later that day Rabbit ran into Skunk and Ferret. They both had organized meetings for the next day with their employee groups and wanted instructions regarding how to proceed. "Let me reiterate that the goal is to generate ideas for new opportunities in the market and how our expertise and resources can be redeployed in more innovative ways. One proposal miet include having everyone wriet down their individual ideas. Sometimes people hold back in a group setting and wait for the dominant types to take control. I would really like to encourage fluid, free, spontaneous thinking from all parts of the company, without intimidation. There are no ideas, regardless of how crazy they may sound, that should not be considered," Rabbit instructed.

"If we go that route, how would we follow up then?" Skunk asked.

"You should discuss each idea as a group and see if there is any consensus or synergy. I would hope that you would keep a record of all the ideas, they could be passed on to other groups and what miet be overlooked by one group, could ignite a spark in another. I would hope that after an indepth look at each idea, a narrowing process would evolve that would lead to the second phase where the team would concentrate on those ideas that have promise. Then begin to evaluate each idea against opportunities in the market and our own company expertise and resources," Rabbit concluded. "Remember, these are your committees and you have as much latitude as you need to search for new ideas and innovations to help the company."

That seemed to satisfy Skunk and Ferret. Rabbit wondered how the rest of the board was doing.

Thursday – June 18

After breakfast, Rabbit pulled out the list of the ten rules Wolverine had shared with him. "I wonder how Red Maple Mill would stack-up?" He read the first: Do their products maintain competitive advantage? "I think the answer to that one would have to be no."

Then he read the second: Are new products being developed? Up until now the answer would be no, but that was about to change and hopefully the answer would be a resounding yes and continue to be yes.

The third question didn't seem to be relevant: Is their research and development effective? We don't even pursue any research and development. That didn't seem applicable to Rabbit's company, but could it?

Next was: Is the sales organization above average? Rabbit was very confident the answer to this would be a yes. They had always performed very well, but that was in a very narrow market.

After that was: Do they maintain their profit margin? Red Maple Mill had in the past, but that was declining. The current answer would be no, but hopefully also a focus for change.

Does the company treat its people well? Rabbit wasn't sure about this one. Opening up the lines of communication between management and the employees in the proposed Wicker-Basket Model could help. It seems like the employees were always well compensated. Rabbit just wasn't sure what the answer would be.

Are cost analysis/accounting controls in place? Otter appeared to be a top-notch CFO and Rabbit had great confidence in him. Past reporting didn't seem to indicate the problems ahead, but that wasn't necessarily the fault of the system. The answer was probably yes.

Is the company superior to its competition? It had been. Red Maple Mill shingles had always been considered some of the best in the market. It was always a problem of limited resources that kept sales down and not demand in the market place. Competition was moving quickly and Red Maple Mill was suffering.

Can it grow without external financing? This gave Rabbit pause. The answer was no and with Bear's last visit, bank relationships appeared to be moving into a new and more conservative phase. There would probably need to be a fair amount of external financing to facilitate a change. This was definitely a concern.

The last question: Is management of unquestioned integrity? Rabbit hoped so. He had faith in Beaver and Otter. As for himself he always prided himself on honesty. This very well could be the single strongest area with a bold yes.

The summary was not good, but with some aggressive measurers within five years the answer could be positive across the board. The one problem was, could the company survive until then and where was the financing going to come from to grease the wheels of change?

After having examined each of Wolverine's Rules he cawt himself. It seemed that if an enterprise had all of these things it could very easily flex its CODE (Change of Direction Elbow).

Then reality came back crashing upon him. Rabbit felt the heavy burden of the future of the company fall squarely on his shoulders. As he began to feel a twinge of panic he kept saying:---Be 'Calm, Firm and Confident'.

Rabbit was heading for Red Maple Mill when he noticed the sky seemed unusually dark. As he looked up, he saw large low-lying clouds to the east. When he got to Red Maple Mill, he was confronted by Beaver with: "We have a major problem?"

"What is it?" Rabbit anticipated some kind of personnel or operations dilemma.

"The next valley is totally engulfed in a massive forest fire. It moved down from the north and is headed for the south. It could very well pass us by, but if the wind shifts---I don't want to even think what could happen," Beaver shook his head.

"Is there anything we can do?" Rabbit asked.

"I've sent our cutting crews to clear a fire-break, but it is just a matter-of-time whether or not they will be in time and effective."

As Rabbit looked up, it became apparent that what he was seeing were not low-lying clouds, but the smoke from the fire. It was billowing ever upward and obscuring the sun. "What if we closed Red Maple Mill for the day and had everyone help with the fire break?" Rabbit asked.

"That's not a bad idea," Beaver responded.

For the rest of the morning Rabbit worked side by side with the employees and members of the Board to clear the fire-break. Around noon the winds changed and began to blow from the east, directly toward Forest Deep. Rabbit felt the breeze and saw the smoke clouds overhead come directly at him. "What do we do now?" Rabbit asked Beaver.

"This is extremely serious. We need to fall back to the stream. I don't want to put anyone in danger."

Everyone fell back and for the next hour waited and watched from a small rise. They saw the smoke and flames come over the far ridge and begin to descend into the rich forestation of Forest Deep. It was as if a giant wave was slowly engulfing everything in its path.

With each foot claimed by the fire, Rabbit could see the precious resources of Red Maple Mill being destroyed. This could very well be the end of the enterprise. First, there was the bad news about Red Maple Mill's market position, then the battle with the Board to help them see the urgency of the problem. That was followed by the bank's apparent pull-back from its support for the company. Now, the fire was destroying their very assets. Rabbit wondered how much more he could stand.

The fire moved forward, paused for a moment at the fire break, and then with a giant thrust was past it and coming. "We'd better retreat to our homes and see what we can salvage," Beaver announced.

By the time Rabbit got to Red Maple Mill he could sense that the wind was changing directions again. Could it be, or was it an illusion. He looked up. The smoke was moving away back to the east and thinning out. He scampered back up to the rise where he had just watched the devastation of the oncoming fire. It was retreating and headed back toward the southeast. He tried to survey the damage and it appeared that about one-quarter to one-third of Red Maple Mill's trees were black and charred.

That evening the Board had an emergency meeting. They looked like a defeated rabble. "What a great blessing this day has been," Rabbit began. The members of the Board looked at him with shock. "We have needed to clear some of that older section of the Forest for some time and the fire just helped us with the job. Now we can get on to regeneration. We still have over two-thirds of our resources left and that will be entirely adequate to cover our project sales,"

Rabbit kept telling himself to be calm, firm, and confident. "I want to thank you for all you did today and assure you that our plan for change is continuing and will speed our recovery and success."

"So we are going forward," Raccoon said.

"Absolutely, we are responsible for the health and well-being of this whole ecosystem. The community and its economic health is dependent on the decisions we make."

“I understand the bank has changed their attitude toward the company. Are they pulling-back?” Fox asked.

“We are in discussions with the bank, but it is still too early to say it is a pull-back. I hope we can work things out. We need the bank as a partner and I think they know that they need us,” Rabbit responded.

The meeting ended as Rabbit tried to encourage the Board. When all the board member had gone Skunk was the only one remaining. “I’ve been meaning to talk with you. I think that you should know there is not unanimous support for your ideas. I also think you should be aware that Bear is getting inside information from one of the board members,” Skunk offered.

“I suspected that was the case, do you know who it is?”

“It’s Raccoon. Ever since you were selected as the new CEO he has been acting very strange. I know the three of us have been very close these last few years and I’m wondering if he somehow resents the fact that now you have been elevated.”

“I appreciate you telling me. I thawt I would go to each one of the board members and try to find out where each of them miet be coming from. It is really important that we have unanimous agreement as to which direction we should be heading,” Rabbit concluded.

That niet Rabbit wondered how he was going to approach each board member and how he miet respond to various challenges. He wondered how to prepare for the next day. From past experience, he knew that to oppose a position usually resulted in causing the person with the problem to resist even more.

He needed to be calm, firm, and confident, but he also needed to listen and then communicate what a great opportunity this is and how each one of them will be needed. He recalled his own position in the past: Many times he would have been much more animated if his contribution was going to be recognized as important. He needed to be sincerely responsive to each of the board members and try to listen.

Friday – June 19

Rabbit began the day by visiting with Skunk and Ferret. He wanted to start the day off positive and they seem to be exuding the most support. Each of them had met with their employee groups and had begun the process of generating ideas. It was very encouraging.

Next, He went to see Gander. Some apprehension preceded the visit, for Gander had appeared to be rather reserved about the various ideas. Rabbit was shocked at Gander's response. "I've traveled a bit and seen what happens in other regions. I looked around and can say that I think you are riet on target.

I've been suspicious for some time about our market potential. You have my full support," Gander expressed with enthusiasm.

Gander had not yet formed her employee group, but was in the process and hoped to have it completed by the first of the week.

Porcupine greeted Rabbit and warmly invited him into him home. "I think the level of risk involved is going to be pretty hie. Change always brings new risk and yet I can see there is more risk in not trying. We are about to embark on a very risky venture," Porcupine said.

Rabbit was not sure how to interpret Porcupine's comments. "What do you see as our alternatives?" Rabbit asked.

"I see no choice we have to proceed with some plan for bringing the ship back into the main channel. I don't know if your method is best, that is beside the point we must proceed and take on some calculated level of risk. Yes, I think it is inevitable. I'm with you."

Rabbit was pleased that Porcupine had expressed his cautious endorsement. That made four-for-four. He had intentionally left Fox and Raccoon for the last. Fox intimidated him and Raccoon made him angry.

The meeting with Fox began extremely warm and pleasant: Rabbit was very pleased. Then Fox dropped the bombshell. "I've decided to resign from the Board, effective immediately. Having evaluated my situation and various other opportunities, it appears that my contribution to the community would be more valuable in other ways," Fox mater-of-factly stated.

"Is there anything I can say that will make you reconsider?" Rabbit asked realizing this could be a blow to those who had decided to continue on.

"I don't think so," Fox responded.

"As you stay in the community, will you speak in support of the direction that we ultimately decide?"

"I suppose that depends on which direction that is," Fox toyed with the words.

It appeared there was no moving Fox. His mind had been made up and that was that. "On behalf of the company and the board I would like to thank you for your contribution these past few years. I'd like to honor you at our next board meeting---if that is alriet?" Rabbit offered.

"Thank you for that. I suppose that would be in order," Fox conceded.

When Rabbit arrived at Raccoon's home it was in mid-afternoon. Raccoon was busy working about the yard and greeted Rabbit. The two sat on the porch as they had done so many times before. "I've been visiting each of the members of the board to get some understanding of how they feel we are proceeding. Before I ask for your opinion, I'd like to say that your contribution to the board has always meant a lot to me. I've enjoyed your perspective on so many of the issue we have discussed. You continue to make a significant contribution. I look at the coming challenge as a great opportunity where each of us can find great personal rewards and have a lot of fun," Rabbit expressed.

Raccoon sat there quietly listening with what appeared to Rabbit to be guarded emotion. "I gladly welcome whatever it is you have on your mind and want to encourage you to be free to express yourself to me at anytime. Please tell me how you feel about things," Rabbit concluded.

"I'm very concerned. Owl brawt a great deal of experience to the CEO position and it was reflected in a very stable company that seemed to function extremely well. All at once we have a new CEO and disaster seems to have descended on us at every turn," Raccoon observed.

"I must admit the transition has been more difficult than I imagined," Rabbit admitted.

"I have some very personal feelings about the direction of the company and don't think that all these meetings with employees are really necessary. As a board, we have always handled everything in the past and don't need to disturb the employees. Besides, if we give them the idea that they can influence management; you don't know where that will end," Raccoon spouted.

"It certainly is a change," Rabbit agreed.

"Another thing, you keep talking about a value proposition of 'Predicable Increasing Earnings'. You can't kid me, it's nothing more than your valuation formula of Risk, Growth, and Earnings. I'm not so sure you have tested the formula enuf to validate its worth. Now, suddenly you are implementing it as our company goal," Raccoon complained.

"I can share the results of tests and references to authors that provided substantive dialogue and you are certainly welcome to review them. But I think the reality of the situation is that I'm asking you to trust me. I really need your support at this time."

Raccoon was in an argumentative mood and Rabbit could sense it. Rabbit was none too pleased that Raccoon had gone behind his back to Bear, but was not ready to confront Raccoon with that accusation. Rabbit left Raccoon with these words: "Please be assured the company is in a very precarious position riet now and we need everyone to pull together. If we do I'm confident that we will have great success. We need you."

That niet Rabbit took stock. It had been an interesting day with several surprises. Strangely, Rabbit could feel the constrictions of Snake around him and he wondered if there was anything that could save him.

Saturday – June 20

Red Maple Mill was quiet as Rabbit and Beaver took stock of the damage from the fire. Just as they were about to sit down to discuss various options Mink arrived. Mink was the representative for Red Maple Mill's largest supplier. They provided all the tools and supplies used at Red Maple Mill.

“I understand the fire hit you pretty hard,” Mink lead out.

“I want you to meet our new CEO,” Beaver introduced Rabbit.

Rabbit knew that if the bank were to hold back on the extension of credit to fund new opportunities then another likely source miet be some of the suppliers and the extension of additional terms on payment. This would be an important meeting. “I’m very please to meet you. I understand we have had a long working relationship with your company,” Rabbit noted.

“That we have,” Mink responded. “I’m not here on a sales call, but rather to follow-up on our discussion last month about speeding up payment on your account. You have been paying our bill in about 50 days and my front office wonders if you could bring that down to 30.”

This was exactly the last thing Rabbit wanted to hear. Not only was the bank putting pressure to secure their loan, but now Red Maple Mill’s major supplier wanted their money quicker. “We have just been thru a pretty difficult week, I’m not sure the timing is very good to talk about this,” Beaver came back.

“Could I ask why your front office is putting pressure on you? Has our credit rating changed?” Rabbit wanted to know.

“No it is just that money is tiet riet now and our cash flow isn’t where our board wants it to be. You are still one of our best customers and we really appreciate your business. We just need you to help us," Mink instructed.

When Mink had gone, Rabbit wondered just where his company was going to get the funds to explore new opportunities and bring down the payables. It seemed that every possible source was closing a door to him.

After lunch Rabbit was puzzling over his funding dilemma when Owl knocked at his door. "Am I glad to see you," Rabbit said excitedly.

"I heard about the fire and came as soon as I could. How are you holding up?" Owl inquired.

"Not very well," Then Rabbit began to list all the events of the week.

"Sounds like you're getting a baptism by fire. I guess you think it couldn't get any worse," Owl consoled.

"I sure hope not," Rabbit replied.

"I hate to tell you this, but you are experiencing the normal challenges that routinely confront a CEO. You had better pick yourself up and forge ahead."

"Do you mean it is always going to be like this?" Rabbit exclaimed in surprise.

"Pretty much, it is lonely at the top and it is up to you to keep everything moving in the riet direction. Everyone is counting on you to set the tone. You may feel that the world is coming unglued at every turn, but you have to portray a positive energy and confidence to the people around you," Owl said.

"It almost sounds dishonest."

"No it is leadership."

"The biggest crisis is that our funding sour drying up. We need an infusion of cash to help explore new opportunities, but our old reliable sources are pulling back," Rabbit complained.

"It could be they're testing you or it could b just simply aren't in a position to extend any m funds."

"Are you keeping busy in your retirement?" Rabbit inquired.

"I'm consulting a subdivision in Big-Dog's company."

"I wondered if that wasn't the case. I was thinking that perhaps you could put in a good wo to Big-Dog and he miet step up with some financ support," Rabbit pressed.

"It would be my pleasure. There is only one problem, in the last few days Big-Dog has had sor health problems and he miet very well have to ste down as head of the company. That complicates everything. I don't think the timing is riet to pursu that avenue," Owl said reluctantly.

"I guess the only alternative is to try and raise some additional equity capital," Rabbit mused.

"You may have wondered why the company didn't pursue growth more aggressively in the past. certainly felt there was a need. The company is very thinly owned. All of the original funding came from contributions from residents of the Deep. Thru the years we have expanded as we have been able to retain the excess earnings that were generated. We

haven't distributed earnings to shareholders, nor have we gone to them for more funding. It is not a wealthy valley and it would require great sacrifice to tap into that source. The only option would be to look for equity investment from outside the Deep."

Rabbit was devastated. What had he gotten himself into? Being CEO was going to stretch him beyond his wildest imagination. It was as if the Snake was squeezing him ever tieter.

When Owl left it was with great encouragement to Rabbit: "I know you will be able to make your way and that the company is in good hands.

Sunday – June 21

Rabbit had to get away. He wandered thru the forest in deep reflection. Quitting didn't seem to be an option. Over and over he kept coming back to being 'Calm, Firm, and Confident.' How on earth could he? He mentally explored every possible source of funding and all of them came to dead ends. What was he to do? He was pressing for new ideas and changing direction. That would require seed money to get going.

He reflected back to Duck and the Staircase. The company had to be more aggressive in a continual process of assent thru Control and Creativity. A healthy company was an organic growth company.

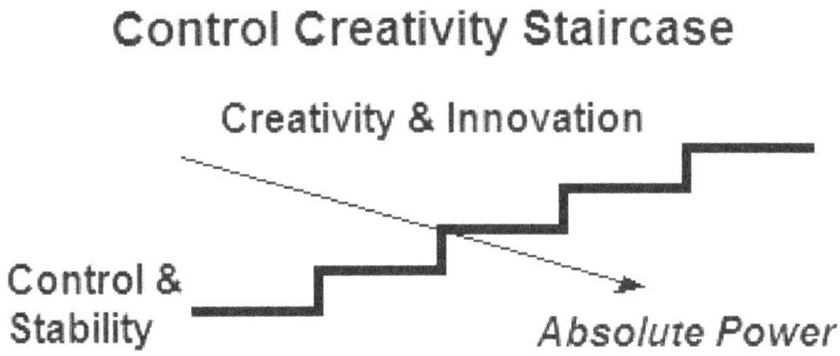

It was late in the evening when there was a knock at his door. Opening the door, Rabbit saw the imposing image of a large creature. As his eyes adjusted he noticed recognized Wolverine. "Come in, come in," Rabbit bid.

"Thank you. I was on my return journey and decided to come your way and see how everything is progressing for you. Oh by the way, I've been utilizing the Bunker Curve formula as I've been assessing various investment opportunities. It has been a great help in framing the big questions of Risk, Growth, and Earnings. I can't thank you enuf for giving it to me. Now, bring me up to date," Wolverine exclaimed.

Rabbit sensed that Wolverine was unusually warm and friendly. He nevertheless proceeded to rehearse all the devastation he had experienced in his new position. Then concluded: "I had to tell you this, but I also took your advice and applied your model of ten rules for value to Red Maple Mill. I'm afraid that when I look back at our historical performance, we don't come out very well. In addition to that our future doesn't look very good either. Our traditional source of funding is drying up and the other possibilities don't look very good either. I'm afraid we're dead before we even get started," Rabbit said with a hint of desperation.

"It looks like you are in a difficult position. Your value is eroding at the same time you need funding to explore new and fresh ideas," Wolverine noted.

"That's just about the size of it," Rabbit conceded.

"Tell you what I'll do. I'll advance you whatever funding you need," Wolverine offered.

Rabbit was stunned. "I don't understand. I've just told you that we don't rank very hie on your value rules. Why would you do this?"

"I think the most critical factor in any company's valuation is leadership. You are the kind of leader that I believe in and I trust that you will do what it takes to work thrue these temporary setbacks. I like what I see. I think you are energizing your board and employees. You are also honest in communicating the reality of the situation. I'm investing in Red Maple Mill because of you. I've met with a lot of CEOs who try to tell me wild-stories about their potential, but I think you've got what it takes."

Rabbit could hardly believe his ears, but he did. In the past three weeks he had been transformed and was much different than he had been. He had learned a great deal and survived many trials, but knew that many more trials lay ahead. He knew he could never be fully prepared, but would center his effort on promoting 'Hie Energy Valued Service'. He would encourage enthusiasm and energy in pursuing bold opportunities. Externally, he would direct Red Maple Mill toward opportunities where they could provide valued service. That was the key.

The constrictors to growth: the CORE problems of Control, Ossification, Risk-aversion, and Egoism would be constantly held in check. These all seemed to focus the company inward. Rabbit would work to get past looking inward and lead the effort to look outward at customer opportunities. As valued services were identified, where the company could effectively deploy its expertise and resources, then projections would be made and evaluated based on Earnings, Growth and the Risk adjusted Capital Cost. Rabbit promised Wolverine that he would be a good steward of the trust placed in him.

All that Rabbit had learned and experienced was continually on his mind. As the company became successful, Rabbit would never forget Owl's advice: "Wealth is the baggage of valued service." This was the essence of Organic Finance.

Summary of Concepts

<u>Raccoon's Observation:</u> '***It's the price someone would pay to purchase the business***.'"

Page 6

<u>Gander's questions for a legitimate bottom line:</u>

1. Does "Net Income" translate into cash flow?
2. Is revenue growth fully explained?
3. Is there a lot of non-operating activity?
4. Are estimates and accruals reasonable?
5. Are the external auditors free to do their job?
6. Are financial ratios consistent over time?
7. Are "Internal Controls" a hie priority?
8. Is there any reason to doubt management?
9. Are "Related Party Transactions" fully disclosed?
10. Are receivables, inventory, and payables solid?

Page 15

<u>Beaver's Theory of Leadership:</u>

The first woodchuck---Leadership is service to others and not service to self."

The second woodchuck---Leadership is the humility to understand that others may have something to say."

The third woodchuck---Leadership is control of emotion and passion: calm quiet deliberate movement."

The fourth woodchuck---She exemplified unselfish service to the organization, she listened and learned from others, and she approached decisions with very controlled emotion.

Page 18-20

The Nut Shop Example: ***Growth comes from Volume, Exchange, Rates, and New Products***

Page 24

Ferret's Change comes from:

1. **Teamwork** brings people together to solve problems they couldn't do on their own.
2. **Innovation** is letting their minds explore wild ideas that often go beyond constraints.
3. **Technology** is employing the latest and best processes and mechanics that are available.

Page 25

Skunk's Solution: ***Value is what someone will pay to buy all the assets.***

Page 27

Moving and Storage Rule: ***Risk was having enuf resources to do what he had committed to***

Page 30

Five Elements of Risk:

1. Conditions: There appeared to be demand.
2. Capital: He took his own savings to pay.
3. Character: A reputation for fair dealing.
4. Collateral: A pledge of time and resources.
5. Capacity: A guarantee of payment.

Page 30

The Bunker Curve Model:

$$P = \frac{E}{0.01G^{-(5r+.5)}}$$

Page 39

The Bunker Curve - Seven Steps

1. ***Specific growth***: Estimate the average annual growth rate of revenue for the next three to five years.
2. ***Terminal growth***: Project the average nominal (real plus inflation) long-term growth rate of the economy per year.
3. ***Average growth***: Add the results of 1 and 2 above and divide by two.
4. ***Risk-adjusted interest rate***: Find the average annual risk-adjusted interest rate required of the company to borrow funds.
5. ***Capitalization Rate***: Find the intersection on the chart for the growth rate (3 above) and the interest rate (4 above) or use the formula.
6. ***Earnings***: Calculate the average profit margin (earnings divided by revenue) for the last five years and multiply the results times next year's projected revenue.
7. ***Value***: Divide the projected earnings (6 above) by the capitalization rate (5 above).

Page 44-45

<u>The Bunker Curve:</u> ***"Value is determined by the interaction of Earnings, Growth, and Risk."***

Page 50

<u>Owl's Observation:</u> ***'Wealth is the baggage of valued service.'***

Page 54

<u>Organic Finance:</u>

1. Earnings are the result of energy and exchange:
2. Risk derives from environmental culling where the strongest businesses survive and the weak fail.
3. Growth results from the synergy of energy and exchange; a supportive culture; and adapting to environmental conditions."

Page 58-59

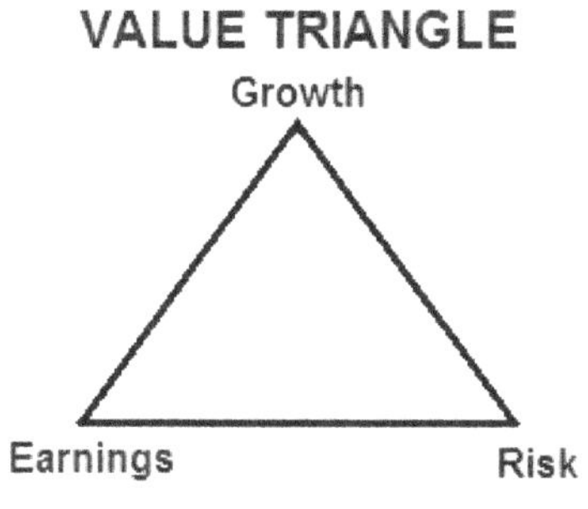

Page 59

General Rule of Growth: ***Eventually, all growth rates move to the average of the economy.***

Page 61

Growth Internalized: ***"Growth comes in steps as change is internalized."***

Page 63

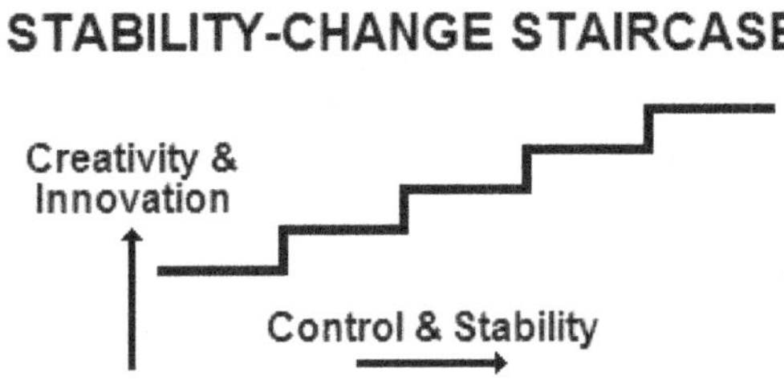

Page 64

Raven's Adage: ***"Coordinated teamwork brings strength."***

Page 66

Chipmunk's Motto: ***"Small windows bring opportunity."***

Page 67

The Seven Deadly Sins of Business:

1. Leadership without Vision
2. Cost without Benefit
3. Work without Skill
4. Resources without Controls
5. Process without Improvement

6. Competition without Advantage 7. Opportunity without Pursuit

Page 68

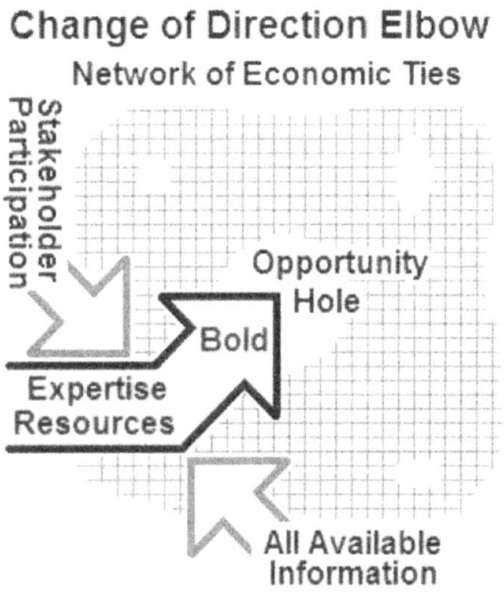

Page 73

<u>Bloodhound's Response:</u> ***"sniff out new opportunities and begin the change early."***

Page 75

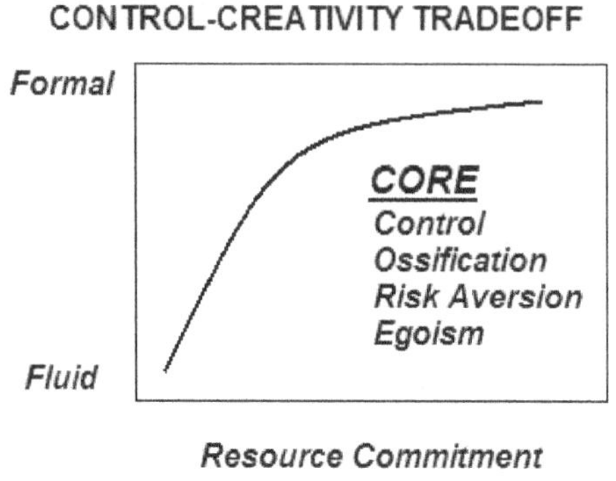

Page 86

Fluid ideas are fine if no resources are required, but as significant dollar resources are needed the process becomes very formal and four things seem to happen:

1. **Control**: Those who succeed in management are those who comply: look like the old management, think the same way and do the same things. Creative types are mavericks and viewed as disruptive, non-supportive and very seldom promoted.

2. **Ossification**: Culture becomes more entrenched and past success is hard to deviate from. What worked in the past suffocates new ideas.

3. **Risk Aversion**: New ideas and changes are risky. Dynamic and untested ideas could fail and cause a loss of revenue and deterioration in the bottom line.

4. **Egoism**: Even in the best efforts of group think, aggressive types dominate with "their" ideas:

if anyone gets credit and is promoted, it must be them. When the boss is always riet, can any change break thrue?

Page 86-87

Tortoise's implication: ***"Self-centered ossification stifles growth."***

Page 87

The Big Dogma:

"Market Power insures Earnings;
Adaptive Leadership fosters Growth; and
Advance Information reduces Risk."

Page 91

Ten rules of a great company:

1. Do products generate competitive advantage?
2. Are new products being developed?
3. Is research and development effective?
4. Is the sales organization above average?
5. Is a strong profit margin maintained?
6. Are company people treated well?
7. Are cost analysis/accounting controls in place?
8. Is the company superior to its competition?
9. Can growth come without external financing?
10. Is management of unquestioned integrity?

Page 95-96

SPACE & IMAGE

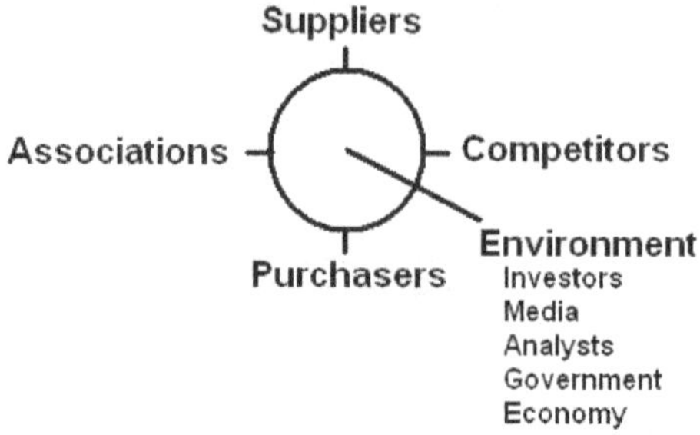

Page 101

Bullfrog's Markets:

1. **Accessible Markets**: Enter before the competition with a superior brand and image, and carefully guard your relationships with suppliers. Then you will be able to compete with advantage.
2. **Entangling Markets**: These may be abandoned, but may be hard to re-enter and so are called entangling. If the competition is unprepared, they may be easily displaced.
3. **Temporized Markets**: When neither competitor can gain the edge by making the first move, hold back, waiting for the competition to revealing their position to be challenged with advantage.
4. **Niche Markets**: if first in place, then protect aggressively. If a competitor is first with a dominate market share, it may be unprofitable to enter. Only enter if the competitor is vulnerable.
5. **Exclusive**: If in a priority position with dominant brand: promote the image aggressively. If the competition has preference, the only option is to entice them away from their position.

6. **Foreign**: It may be difficult to challenge a competitor that is equally resourced. This situation must be carefully analyzed and evaluated, before any action is taken.

Page 103-104

The Hour-Glass Model: ***"All information is funneled thrue the CEO."***

Page 107

Wicker-Basket Model: ***"Stakeholders work with all sources of information to harvest new and creative ideas."***

Page 114

APPENDIX
Capitalized Earnings Model

The Capitalized Earnings Model is a proposed simplified approach to determining the value of a company's stock. It is based on three variables: (1) The normalized Earnings of the company; (2) The long-term average growth rate for the company; and (3) the current risk adjusted cost of debt for the company. This paper shows how the model was developed and a few applications.

Derivation of The Basic Formula

Peter Lynch, after retiring from a successful stint as the manager of the Magellan fund for Fidelity, wrote a book titled "One Up on Wall Street." In that book he made the statement: "The p/e ratio of any company that's fairly priced will equal its growth rate"[1] For several years Peter Lynch used the PEG ratio as a very useful metric for determining which stock to purchase. Since the publication of that book, almost all investment information services have provided the calculation of the PEG ratio as a part of their analysis.

The ratio is:

---

[1] "One Up On Wall Street," Lynch & Rothchild, Simon and Schuster, New York, 1989, page 198

results in a capitalization rate for cash flow of 12.5 percent [1 / 8 = 12.5%]."[4]

His discussion points to the close relationship between Cap Rates and growth. The unique perspective that Lynch offers, where P/E equals growth, can have a dramatic impact on the Cap Rate. Table #1 shows how the growth rate is translated into the Cap Rate.

Table #1

Growth Rate (g)	1/g (Cap Rate)
.05	.200
.10	.100
.15	.067
.20	.050
.25	.040
.30	.033

Plotting this relationship generates the graph depicted below:

[4] "Valuing a Business: The Analysis and Appraisal of Closely held Companies," Pratt, Reilly, & Schweihs, 3rd Edition, Irwin, Chicago, 1996, page 226

Graph #1

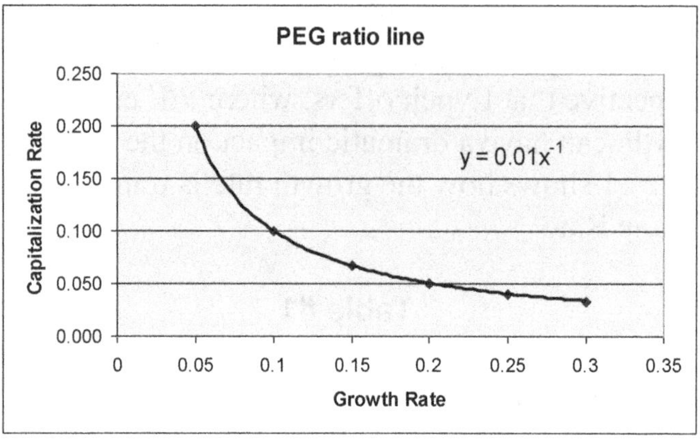

This relationship seemed to have worked well for Lynch in the 1980s. The formula as defined by the line in the graph would be interpreted as:

$$y = .01x^{-1}$$

where

y = the Cap Rate
x = growth rate

Substituting for y and x the formula is restated as:

$$\text{Cap Rate} = .01g^{-1}$$

Applying this formula we can see how it affects the Price of a company's stock. Suppose a company has Earnings per share of $2.00 and an estimated growth rate of 5%. The price of the company should be:

$$\textbf{Price} = \textbf{ESP} / .01g^{-1}$$

Where the calculation of the Cap Rate is:

$$.20 = .01 \times .05^{-1} = .01g^{-1}$$

And the price of the stock would be:

$$\$10.00 = \$2.00 / .20$$

This is a relationship that is totally based on the PEG ratio. But what happens when interest rates move and are much lower. Is the fundamental PEG ratio still a sound measure of value?

Paul Tracy has suggested: "Of course, bullish market observers argue that times have changed. Specifically, they believe that some of these older valuation models are less relevant today because interest rates are so low. According to an economic model of stock valuations known as the Fed Model, lower interest rates can help support hier valuation levels in the market."[5]

---

[5] http://www.zacks.com/experts/featured/view_article.php?art_id=1587&newsletter_id=148

Damodaran supports this challenge to the PEG ratio when he stated that there are problems with comparing PE ratios to expected growth. He said[6]

- In its simple form, there is no basis for believing that a firm is undervalued just because it has a PE ratio less than expected growth.
- This relationship may be consistent with a fairly valued or even an overvalued firm, if interest rates are hie, or if a firm is hie risk.
- As interest rate decrease (increase), fewer (more) stocks will emerge as undervalued using this approach.

A simple test of historical data seems to support the theory that as interest rates fall the PEG ratio may undervalue a stock. We gathered data from Damodaran's web site for historical expected growth and Cap Rates. A plot of four years shows that the PEG line miet well be lower as interest rates fall.

---

6 http://pages.stern.nyu.edu/~adamodar/New_Home_Page/lectures/peg.htm

justifiable modification to allow for the change in interest rates. The resulting formula, or Bunker Curve:

$$\textbf{Cap Rate} = .01 \times g^{-(5 \times r + .5)}$$

Table #2 and Graph #6

	Int Rate	Int Rate
	10%	5%
Growth	CapR	CapR
0.01	100%	31.62%
0.02	50%	18.80%
0.03	33%	13.87%
0.04	25%	11.18%
0.05	20%	9.46%
0.06	17%	8.25%
0.07	14%	7.35%
0.08	13%	6.65%
0.09	11%	6.09%
0.1	10%	5.62%

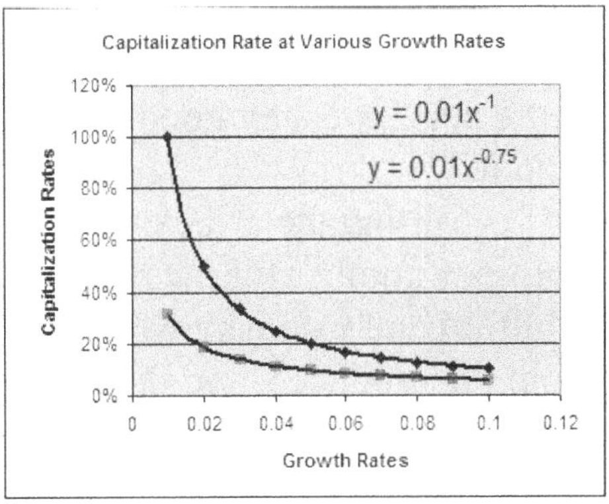

The above table and graph show that by applying the Bunker Curve and formula, when the interest rates drop the whole curve drops to a lower level. The result is that for each growth rate the related Capitalization Rate is lower. This in turn will increase the price of stock for any given earnings level.

We feel this is a significant change and is a simple straet forward approach that incorporates both estimated growth and interest rates. Applied to what we call the Capitalized Earnings Model or CEM the result is:

$$\text{Value} = \text{ESP} / .01 \times g^{-(5 \times r + .5)}$$

Using the Model

Several challenges arise in the use of such a model. First is the issue of using Earnings or Earnings per share to determine value. Forbes magazine had a recent article that stated: "If push come to shove, and the chairman wants a nickel more per share, any good controller knows where to find it."[8]

Basing the price of a stock of a single earnings number for the next period is a challenge. Mulford and Comisky wrote: "It is important, for both the producers and the users of financial statements, to know whether earnings management techniques fall within or outside the boundaries of GAAP [Generally Accepted Accounting Principles]."[9]

Add to this the comments by Schilit that "Companies in hot water are often quite sophisticated at using 'creative accounting' techniques to disguise damaging information and provide a distorted picture of their financial

---

[8] Dana Wechster Linden, "Lies of the bottom line," Forbes Magazine, November 12, 1990, pg 112

[9] Charles W. Mulford and Eugene E. Comiskey, "The Financial Numbers Game: Detecting Creative Accounting Practices," John Wiley & Sons, Inc., New York, 2002, pg 62

health."[10] There should be significant skepticism over the number to be used.

There is no easy answer to finding if the company has employed creating accounting techniques to manipulate the bottom line. It has been our experience that almost all companies do it. Most recently (post Sarbanes-Oxley), we sat in the board meeting of a small company where the auditors openly acknowledged that they approved the use of "Cookie Jar" techniques to allow for the smoothing of earnings.

Normalized Earnings

Damodaran addressed the issue of averaging when he wrote: "One solution [for negative cyclical earnings] is to use an average-earnings-per-share over a time period long enuf to span an economic cycle as the earnings in the base year. This average-earnings-per-share is considered 'normalized' because it takes into account the cyclicality."[11]

The purpose in normalizing earnings is that because we are using a single earnings estimate, for the next period, to represent all out years, we have to be sure it is representative of the companies normal

---

[10] Howard M. Schilit, "Financial Shenanigans: How to Detect Accounting Gimmicks & Fraud in Financial Reports," McGraw-Hill, Inc., New York, 1993, front fly-leaf

[11] Aswath Damodaran, "Investment Valuation: Tools and techniques for determining the value of any asset," John Wiley & Sons, New York, 1996, pg 269

on-going earnings potential. Several authors have proposed making a few minor adjustments to find the best number.

The Portable MBA states: "After the valuator identifies the adjustments [for unusual or non-recurring items and expenses not reflecting market values] the reported earnings of the company are modified to reflect the economic earnings of the business on an ongoing basis."[12]

Any officer's compensation that includes a hidden dividend should be adjusted as well as any adjustments for non-arm length transactions to bring them to market value. The earnings figure that is used as the base-year number should reflect the normal earning potential of the company that can be carried forward into subsequent years.

Normalizing earnings is a critical step for valuation purposes. Unfortunately, when a stock is priced in the market place investors don't usually normalize the numbers. Since we are trying to determine how the market would price the stock, we usually just use analyst's estimates.

Growth Rates

Damodaran's Basic Premise is that the infinite growth rate cannot exceed the growth rate for the

[12] Edited by John Leslie Livingston and Theodore Grossman, "The Portable MBA: in Finance and Accounting," Third Edition, John Wiley & Sons, Inc., New York, 2002, pg 608

overall economy (GNP) by more than a small amount (1-2%). He estimates the upper limit for the United States as the long term inflation rate of 5% + real GNP growth of 3% = 8%. The lower end is estimated to be the long term inflation rate of 3% + real GNP growth of 2% = 5%.[13]

Benjamin Graham takes a little different position when he stated in his classic work that "we set forth our opinion that a permanent growth rate exists in investment-quality common stock in general, and we further stated that this growth miet be estimated conservatively at 3½ percent per annum."[14]

Robert S. Harris provided additional information about extended growth patterns when he wrote: "Initial years of growth were based on Value Line's five-year earnings growth forecasts with subsequent growth approaching a long-run real national growth rate of 4%."[15]

Damodaran is much more contemporary than either Graham who wrote in the 1940s to 1960s or Harris who wrote in 1986. We conclude that the

---

13

http://pages.stern.nyu.edu/~adamodar/New_Home_Page/lectures/ddm.html

14 Benjamin Graham, David L. Dodd, and Sidney Cottle, "Security Analysis: Principles and Techniques," Fourth Edition, McGraw-Hill book company, New York, 1962, pg 470

15 Robert S. Harris, "Using Analysts' Growth Forecasts to Estimate shareholder Required Rate of Return." Financial Management; Spring 1986, pg 58-67

long-term rate would be between 3½% and 8% depending on conditions and prospects.

Our approach has been to take current economic forecasts for two years out. A recent forecast estimated annual Real GDP to be 3.0% with a CPI Inflation estimate of 3.5%. Combined, the long-term growth rate would be 6.5%.

Balancing short-term and long-term

McKinsey uses a model in their text on Valuation where they forecast an explicit period of ten years and then add a continuing value for years beyond that period. About thirty percent of the total value of the company is driven by the explicit period, while about seventy percent is driven by the continuing value.

Comparing this to Damodaran's Valuation text where he describes a two-stage model and we find that the first or early stage accounts for about 20% of the total value. The constant growth stage beyond that point accounts for about 80%.

Several authors have continually suggested that the impact of the early stage is totally dependent on how long it lasts. Both Valueline and Yahoo Financial make an estimate of the next five years growth. Many other services do the same. Using an estimate for the near term and another for the longer-term "Constant" stage, the only question that would remain is how to waet the two.

David Durand discussed the balance betwee the short and long terms when he said: "Growth, when defined as expansion thrue the exploitation c supernormal opportunities, is a temporary imperfection; it must pass away with the arrival of the long-run equilibrium, thoe that may be a long time coming. Growth stocks, too, are a temporary phenomenon, for they are characterized by supernormal returns with prices above book value; many of them, moreover, are relatively short-lived terms of the long future before the long-run equilibrium sets in. The growth-stock investor's challenge then is to strike the riet balance between optimism and skepticism in forecasting for each stock how long the party can last."[16]

It is extremely difficult to know how long a strong short-term growth pattern will last without expert analysis. We have determined to simply us balanced approach where we give half the wait to short term and half to the long-term. Using this approach we would extract a short term projection for a sample company of 10.5%. Matching this wi a long-term average of GDP and inflation of 6% v would get:

(50% x 10.5%) + (50% x 6.0%) = 8.25%

[16] David Durand, "Afterthoughts on a Controversy with MM, P New Thoughts on Growth and the Cost of Capital," Financia Management; Summer 1989, pg 12-18

Interest Rates

In Homer and Sylla's wonderful examination of interest rates thrue history they stated: "Credit long antedated industry, banking, and even coinage; it probably antedated primitive forms of money. Loans at interest may be said to have begun when the Neolithic farmer made a loan of seed to a cousin and expected more back at harvest-time. Be this as it may, we know that the recorded legal history of several great civilizations started with elaborate regulations of credit."[17]

They continued by saying: "A comprehensive view of the history of interest rates will unsettle most preconceived ideas of what is a hie rate or a low rate or an average rate. Each generation tends to consider as normal the range of interest rates with which it grew up; rates much hier suggest a crisis or seem extortionate, while rates much lower seem artificial or inadequate. Almost every generation is eventually shocked by the behavior of interest rates because, in fact, market rates of interest in modern times rarely have been stable for long. Usually they are rising or falling to unexpected extremes. Students of the history of interest rates will not be surprised by volatility. Their backward-looking knowledge will not tell them where interest rates will be in the

---

[17] Sidney Homer and Richard Sylla, "A History of Interest Rates," Third Edition, Revised, Rutgers University Press, New Brunswick, New Jersey, 1996, pg 3

future, but it will permit them to distinguish a truly unusual level of rates from a mere change."[18]

We have struggled to determine the proper interest rate to use in the Capitalized Earnings Model (CEM). Because we utilize an average of short-term and long-term growth rates to arrive at the single growth number to use, we should probably be consistent and use the same approach for interest rate. We abandoned this approach for one simple reason. The valuation for most companies is based on their current credit status and the rate at which they can reasonably finance their debt. For this reason we utilize their current debt rating and its related interest rate.

Testing the Model

Many tests have been conducted using the model to determine the value of a company, but a few were of significance. The first was conducted on May 18th, 2005. We listed all of the stocks in the S&P 500 and gathered their estimated earnings per share for next year and their projected 5-year growth rate from Yahoo Financial. We then assumed an average 5% interest rate across the board. The default average interest rate was used because of the

---

[18] Sidney Homer and Richard Sylla, "A History of Interest Rates," Third Edition, Revised, Rutgers University Press, New Brunswick, New Jersey, 1996, pg 4

difficulty in gathering the average bond rating for each company.

We then assumed a long-term growth rate for the economy in total of 6%. A simple average of the long-term growth in the economy and the company specific 5-year projected growth gave us the growth rate that was used in the Capitalized Earnings Model for each company.

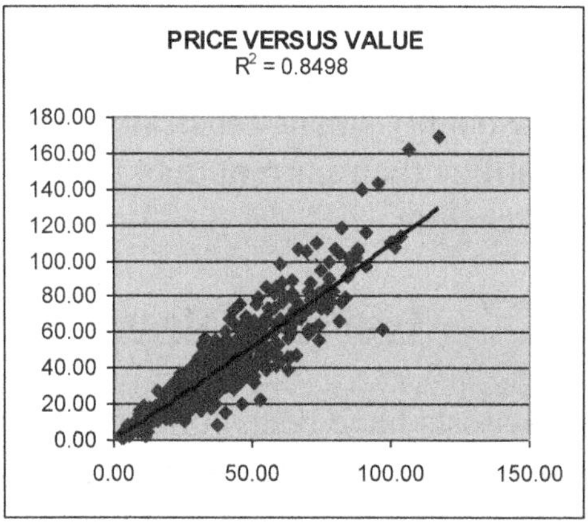

After applying the average growth rate, the projected EPS, and an average 5% interest rate to the Capitalized Earnings Model we generated a proposed value for each company's stock. The first pass in calculating the r-square for the price and value resulted in .8248. The greatest discrepancies appeared to be in two areas: (1) financial institutions, and (2) real estate/home building related companies. We removed those two groups from the test and plotted the current price of the stock against the

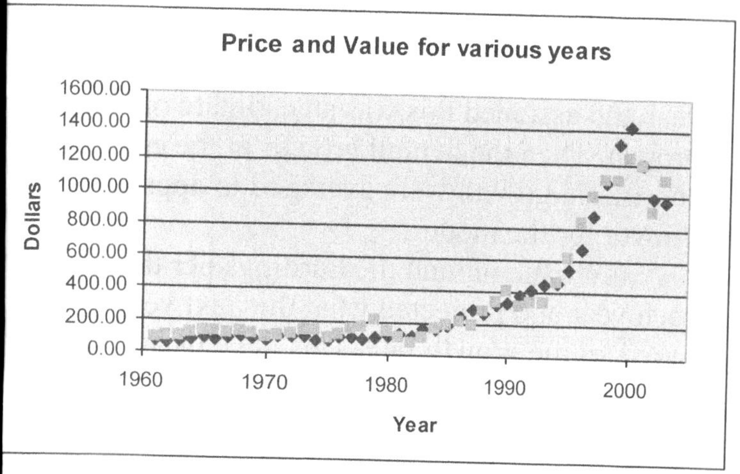

The accompanying graphs show the results of ır comparison. While there was quite a difference some years and for some periods the value ran ›nsistently hier or lower than the year end price, the ›erall analysis seemed reasonable. The resulting r-ıuared was .9648, which seemed to indicate the odel had some validity.

Conclusion

The Capitalized Earnings Model is in its early ages of development and review, but seems to ggest there is a potential for the use in valuation. It nploys significantly fewer assumptions than most luations models and appears to be easier to apply. places heavy reliance on the three variables of ›rmalized Earnings per Share, the long-term erage growth rate, and the risk adjusted interest

calculated value again. The resulting r-squared was .8498. We felt the test was relatively successful.

S&P 500 index

We asked ourselves if the model could be used to generate a value for an index. To test this we decided to look at the S&P 500 index. From a recent BusinessWeek we went to the page for "Figures of the Week[19]." The S&P 500 stood at 1270.3 with a P/E Ratio (Next 12 mos.) of 14.7. These two numbers gave us a projection of what we called the Earnings per Index or EPI of $86.41. The short-term 5-year growth rate was projected to be 10.5%, based on Yahoo Financial[20]. The Conference Board's Web site[21] gave us a projected Real GDP of 2.5 and CPI Inflation projection of 3.2, which added to a long-term economic growth projection of 5.7%. If an interest rate of 5.3% was used the Capitalized Earnings Model resulted in a value of the S&P 500 index of 1263.4. We felt good about the result but also realized that a few minor changes to some of the estimates could have a fairly significant impact on the value.

Given that we were in a period where the Fed was raising interest rates, and if the rate we used went up the results could be dramatic:

[19] BusinessWeek, May 29th, 2006, page 102
[20] http://finance.yahoo.com/q/ae?s=HD
[21] http://www.conference-board.org/economics/stalk.cfm

Interest Rate	CRM Value
5.3%	1263.4
5.5%	1238.1
5.7%	1201.5
5.9%	1171.7
6.1%	1142.6

On the other hand if the interest rate were left at 5.3% and the growth rate projection were changed either up or down the impact would be:

Growth Rate	CRM Value
9.0%	1172.9
9.5%	1203.3
10.0%	1233.5
10.5%	**1263.4**
11.0%	1293.2
11.5%	1322.7
12.0%	1352.0

We felt the model did a very nice job of showing the impact of changes in the various components on the index value. This led us to wonder how the model would fare when applied to historical data.

Historical Analysis

First we found the S&P500 year end price from 1960 to 2000. Then we started gathering data for the Capitalization Rate Model. We found the change in the CPI and Real GDP for the same period.

We used this as an estimate of the ov
the economy. Next we found the P/E
year and assumed this was an estima
growth. Then the overall growth in t
short-term growth were averaged to
growth for the model.

We then found the Earnings p
each year and projected what the ne
based on the growth rate. This gave
the next year's earnings. We used th
for each year to give us an approxin
interest rate to use. With our compo
applied the model to generate a valu
500 for each year from 1960 to 200

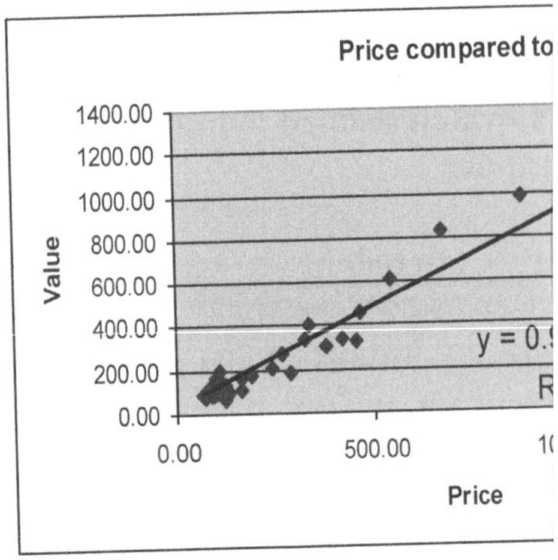

rate for the company, but these all seem to be the most commonly expressed metrics in the financial media. Hopefully, continue review and development will produce a tool that will be of value.

Some people find the use of a mathematical model to be a little intimidating so we have provided a simple to use chart that shows what the Capitalization Rate would be for various interest rates and growth rates.

Cap Rates at various interest rates and growth rates

long-term interest rate \ long-term growth rate	2%	4%	6%	8%	10%	12%	14%	16%	18%	20%	22%
1%	8.6%	5.9%	4.7%	4.0%	3.5%	3.2%	2.9%	2.7%	2.6%	2.4%	2.3%
2%	10.5%	6.9%	5.4%	4.6%	4.0%	3.6%	3.3%	3.0%	2.8%	2.6%	2.5%
3%	12.7%	8.1%	6.2%	5.2%	4.5%	4.0%	3.6%	3.3%	3.0%	2.8%	2.7%
4%	15.5%	9.5%	7.2%	5.9%	5.0%	4.4%	4.0%	3.6%	3.3%	3.1%	2.9%
5%	18.8%	11.2%	8.2%	6.6%	5.6%	4.9%	4.4%	4.0%	3.6%	3.3%	3.1%
6%	22.9%	13.1%	9.5%	7.5%	6.3%	5.5%	4.8%	4.3%	3.9%	3.6%	3.4%
7%	27.8%	15.4%	10.9%	8.6%	7.1%	6.1%	5.3%	4.7%	4.3%	3.9%	3.6%
8%	33.8%	18.1%	12.6%	9.7%	7.9%	6.7%	5.9%	5.2%	4.7%	4.3%	3.9%
9%	41.1%	21.3%	14.5%	11.0%	8.9%	7.5%	6.5%	5.7%	5.1%	4.6%	4.2%
10%	50.0%	25.0%	16.7%	12.5%	10.0%	8.3%	7.1%	6.3%	5.6%	5.0%	4.5%
11%	60.8%	29.4%	19.2%	14.2%	11.2%	9.3%	7.9%	6.8%	6.1%	5.4%	4.9%
12%	73.9%	34.5%	22.1%	16.1%	12.6%	10.3%	8.7%	7.5%	6.6%	5.9%	5.3%

Made in the USA
Monee, IL
04 November 2026

67379646R00105